MznLnx

Missing Links Exam Preps

Exam Prep for

Rethinking the Rules of Financial Accounting

Anthony, 1st Edition

The MznLnx Exam Prep is your link from the texbook and lecture to your exams.
The MznLnx Exam Preps are unauthorized and comprehensive reviews of your textbooks.

All material provided by MznLnx and Rico Publications (c) 2010
Textbook publishers and textbook authors do not particpate in or contribute to these reviews.

MznLnx

Rico Publications

Exam Prep for Rethinking the Rules of Financial Accounting
1st Edition
Anthony

Publisher: Raymond Houge
Assistant Editor: Michael Rouger
Text and Cover Designer: Lisa Buckner
Marketing Manager: Sara Swagger
Project Manager, Editorial Production: Jerry Emerson
Art Director: Vernon Lowerui

Product Manager: Dave Mason
Editorial Assitant: Rachel Guzmanji
Pedagogy: Debra Long
Cover Image: Jim Reed/Getty Images
Text and Cover Printer: City Printing, Inc.
Compositor: Media Mix, Inc.

(c) 2010 Rico Publications

ALL RIGHTS RESERVED. No part of this work covered by the copyright may be reproduced or used in any form or by an means--graphic, electronic, or mechanical, including photocopying, recording, taping, Web distribution, information storage, and retrieval systems, or in any other manner--without the written permission of the publisher.

Printed in the United States
ISBN:

For more information about our products, contact us at:
Dave.Mason@RicoPublications.com

For permission to use material from this text or product, submit a request online to:
Dave.Mason@RicoPublications.com

Contents

CHAPTER 1
Introduction — 1
CHAPTER 2
Criteria — 15
CHAPTER 3
The Financial Position Statement — 28
CHAPTER 4
The Income Statement — 46
CHAPTER 5
Statement of Changes in Equity — 57
CHAPTER 6
The Cash Flow Statement — 62
CHAPTER 7
Nonprofit Accounting — 68
CHAPTER 8
State and Local Government Accounting — 74
CHAPTER 9
Implementation — 83
CHAPTER 10
Federal Accounting Standards — 95
CHAPTER 11
Summary of Recommendations — 100
ANSWER KEY — 105

TO THE STUDENT

COMPREHENSIVE

The *MznLnx* Exam Prep series is designed to help you pass your exams. Editors at MznLnx review your textbooks and then prepare these practice exams to help you master the textbook material. Unlike study guides, workbooks, and practice tests provided by the texbook publisher and textbook authors, *MznLnx* gives you **all** of the material in each chapter in exam form, not just samples, so you can be sure to nail your exam.

MECHANICAL

The MznLnx Exam Prep series creates exams that will help you learn the subject matter as well as test you on your understanding. Each question is designed to help you master the concept. Just working through the exams, you gain an understanding of the subject--its a simple mechanical process that produces success.

INTEGRATED STUDY GUIDE AND REVIEW

MznLnx is not just a set of exams designed to test you, its also a comprehensive review of the subject content. Each exam question is also a review of the concept, making sure that you will get the answer correct without having to go to other sources of material. You learn as you go! Its the easiest way to pass an exam.

HUMOR

Studying can be tedious and dry. MznLnx's instructional design includes moderate humor within the exam questions on occassion, to break the tedium and revitalize the brain

Chapter 1. Introduction

1. The _____ is a private, not-for-profit organization whose primary purpose is to develop generally accepted accounting principles (GAAP) within the United States in the public's interest. The Securities and Exchange Commission (SEC) designated the _____ as the organization responsible for setting accounting standards for public companies in the U.S. It was created in 1973, replacing the Accounting Principles Board and the Committee on Accounting Procedure of the American Institute of Certified Public Accountants. The _____'s mission is 'to establish and improve standards of financial accounting and reporting for the guidance and education of the public, including issuers, auditors, and users of financial information.'

The _____ is not a governmental body.

   a. Public company
   b. Governmental Accounting Standards Board
   c. Financial Accounting Standards Board
   d. Fannie Mae

2. _____ is an umbrella term which refers to the various accounting systems used by various public sector entities. In the United States, for instance, there are two levels of government which follow different accounting standards set forth by independent, private sector boards. At the federal level, the Federal Accounting Standards Advisory Board (FASAB) sets forth the accounting standards to follow.
   a. Management accounting
   b. Product control
   c. Nonassurance services
   d. Governmental Accounting

3. The _____ is currently the source of generally accepted accounting principles (GAAP) used by State and Local governments in the [[United States of America]]. As with most of the entities involved in creating GAAP in the United States, it is a private, non-governmental organization.

The _____ is subject to oversight by the Financial Accounting Foundation (FAF), which selects the members of the _____ and the Financial Accounting Standards Board, and funds both organizations.

   a. National Conference of Commissioners on Uniform State Laws
   b. Multinational corporation
   c. Fannie Mae
   d. Governmental Accounting Standards Board

4. A _____ is a fungible, negotiable instrument representing financial value. they are broadly categorized into debt securities (such as banknotes, bonds and debentures), and equity securities; e.g., common stocks. The company or other entity issuing the _____ is called the issuer.

a. Tracking stock
b. BMC Software, Inc.
c. 3M Company
d. Security

5. The U.S. _____ is an independent agency of the United States government which holds primary responsibility for enforcing the federal securities laws and regulating the securities industry, the nation's stock and options exchanges, and other electronic securities markets. The SEC was created by section 4 of the Securities Exchange Act of 1934 (now codified as 15 U.S.C. §Â§ 78d and commonly referred to as the 1934 Act.)

a. BNSF Railway
b. BMC Software, Inc.
c. 3M Company
d. Securities and Exchange Commission

6. An _____ is a practitioner of accountancy, which is the measurement, disclosure or provision of assurance about financial information that helps managers, investors, tax authorities and other decision makers make resource allocation decisions.

The word '_____' is derived from the French 'Compter' which took its origin from the Latin 'Computare'. The word was formerly written in English as 'Accomptant', but in process of time the word, which was always pronounced by dropping the 'p', became gradually changed both in pronunciation and in orthography to its present form.

a. AMEX
b. ABC Television Network
c. Accountant
d. AIG

7. The _____ is the national, professional association of CPAs in the United States, with more than 330,000 members, including CPAs in business and industry, public practice, government, and education; student affiliates; and international associates. It sets ethical standards for the profession and U.S. auditing standards for audits of private companies; federal, state and local governments; and non-profit organizations.

Approximately 40% of its members are engaged in the practice of public accounting, in areas such as auditing, accounting, taxation, general business consulting, business valuation, personal financial planning and business technology.

Chapter 1. Introduction

a. ABC Television Network
b. American Institute of Certified Public Accountants
c. Other postemployment benefits
d. AIG

8. _____ is the statutory title of qualified accountants in the United States who have passed the Uniform _____ Examination and have met additional state education and experience requirements for certification as a _____. Individuals who have passed the Exam but have not either accomplished the required on-the-job experience or have previously met it but in the meantime have lapsed their continuing professional education are, in many states, permitted the designation '_____ Inactive' or an equivalent phrase. In most U.S. states, only _____s who are licensed are able to provide to the public attestation (including auditing) opinions on financial statements.

a. Certified Public Accountant
b. Certified General Accountant
c. Chartered Accountant
d. Chartered Certified Accountant

9. In economics, a _____ is a mechanism that allows people to easily buy and sell (trade) financial securities (such as stocks and bonds), commodities (such as precious metals or agricultural goods), and other fungible items of value at low transaction costs and at prices that reflect the efficient-market hypothesis.

They have evolved significantly over several hundred years and are undergoing constant innovation to improve liquidity.

Both general markets (where many commodities are traded) and specialized markets (where only one commodity is traded) exist.

a. Mark-to-market
b. Spot rate
c. Transfer agent
d. Financial Market

10. A _____ is any one of a variety of different systems, institutions, procedures, social relations and infrastructures whereby persons trade, and goods and services are exchanged, forming part of the economy. It is an arrangement that allows buyers and sellers to exchange things. _____s vary in size, range, geographic scale, location, types and variety of human communities, as well as the types of goods and services traded.

a. Market Failure
b. Perfect competition
c. Recession
d. Market

11. In business and accounting, _____ are everything of value that is owned by a person or company. It is a claim on the property your income of a borrower. The balance sheet of a firm records the monetary value of the _____ owned by the firm.
   a. Accounts receivable
   b. Earnings before interest, taxes, depreciation and amortization
   c. Accrual basis accounting
   d. Assets

12. _____ and credit are formal bookkeeping and accounting terms. They are the most fundamental concepts in accounting, representing the two records that one party in a transaction makes on its records, transferring a money balance from one account to another, one representing a reduction of liability or increase in asset, and the other representing a balancing increase in liability or reduction of asset.

Introduction

_____s and credits are a system of notation used in accounting to keep track of money movements (transactions) into and out of an account.

   a. Debit and credit
   b. Cookie jar accounting
   c. Debit
   d. Bookkeeping

13. In financial accounting, a _____ is defined as an obligation of an entity arising from past transactions or events, the settlement of which may result in the transfer or use of assets, provision of services or other yielding of economic benefits in the future.
   a. Liability
   b. Corporate governance
   c. Vested
   d. False Claims Act

Chapter 1. Introduction

14. The _____ founded on April 1, 2001 is the successor of the International Accounting Standards Committee (IASC) founded in June 1973 in London. It is responsible for developing the International Financial Reporting Standards (new name for the International Accounting Standards issued after 2001), and promoting the use and application of these standards.

The _____ is an independent, privately-funded accounting standard-setter based in London, UK.

   a. Institute of Management Accountants
   b. Emerging technologies
   c. Information Systems Audit and Control Association
   d. International Accounting Standards Board

15. The _____ is the global organization for the accountancy profession. IFAC has 157 member bodies and associates in 123 countries and jurisdictions, representing more than 2.5 million accountants employed in public practice, industry and commerce, government, and academe. The organization, through its independent standard-setting boards, establishes international standards on ethics, auditing and assurance, education, and public sector accounting.

   a. International Accounting Standards Committee
   b. American Payroll Association
   c. Emerging technologies
   d. International Federation of Accountants

16. The general definition of an _____ is an evaluation of a person, organization, system, process, project or product. _____s are performed to ascertain the validity and reliability of information; also to provide an assessment of a system's internal control. The goal of an _____ is to express an opinion on the person/organization/system (etc) in question, under evaluation based on work done on a test basis.

   a. Assurance service
   b. Institute of Chartered Accountants of India
   c. Audit
   d. Audit regime

17. In financial accounting, a _____ or statement of financial position is a summary of a person's or organization's balances. Assets, liabilities and ownership equity are listed as of a specific date, such as the end of its financial year. A _____ is often described as a snapshot of a company's financial condition.

   a. Balance sheet
   b. Statement of retained earnings
   c. 3M Company
   d. Financial statements

Chapter 1. Introduction

18. The _____ is a performance management tool which began as a concept for measuring whether the smaller-scale operational activities of a company are aligned with its larger-scale objectives in terms of vision and strategy.

By focusing not only on financial outcomes but also on the operational, marketing and developmental inputs to these, the _____ helps provide a more comprehensive view of a business, which in turn helps organizations act in their best long-term interests. This tool is also being used to address business response to climate change and greenhouse gas emissions.

   a. Trustee
   b. Best practice
   c. Management by objectives
   d. Balanced scorecard

19. _____ is a legally declared inability or impairment of ability of an individual or organization to pay its creditors. Creditors may file a _____ petition against a debtor ('involuntary _____') in an effort to recoup a portion of what they are owed or initiate a restructuring. In the majority of cases, however, _____ is initiated by the debtor (a 'voluntary _____' that is filed by the bankrupt individual or organization.)

   a. Bankruptcy
   b. Bankruptcy protection
   c. BMC Software, Inc.
   d. 3M Company

20. _____ are formal records of a business' financial activities.

In British English, including United Kingdom company law, _____ are often referred to as accounts, although the term _____ is also used, particularly by accountants.

_____ provide an overview of a business' financial condition in both short and long term.

   a. 3M Company
   b. Notes to the financial statements
   c. Financial statements
   d. Statement of retained earnings

21. _____ is a company's financial statement that indicates how the revenue is transformed into the net income The purpose of the _____ is to show managers and investors whether the company made or lost money during the period being reported.

The important thing to remember about an _____ is that it represents a period of time.

a. Income statement
b. AIG
c. AMEX
d. ABC Television Network

22. _____ is the process whereby an organization establishes the parameters within which programs, investments, and acquisitions are reaching the desired results. Performance Reference Model of the Federal Enterprise Architecture, 2005.

This process of measuring performance often requires the use of statistical evidence to determine progress toward specific defined organizational objectives.

There are many types of measurements.

a. Trustee
b. Management by objectives
c. Performance measurement
d. Management by exception

23. _____ are financial statements that factor the holding company's subsidiaries into its aggregated accounting figure. It is a representation of how the holding company is doing as a group. The consolidated accounts should provide a true and fair view of the financial and operating conditions of the group.

a. Redemption value
b. Committee on Accounting Procedure
c. Replacement cost
d. Consolidated financial statements

24. _____ s are cash, evidence of an ownership interest in an entity or deliver, cash or another _____ .

_____ s can be categorized by form depending on whether they are cash instruments or derivative instruments:

- Cash instruments are _____ s whose value is determined directly by markets. They can be divided into securities, which are readily transferable, and other cash instruments such as loans and deposits, where both borrower and lender have to agree on a transfer.
- Derivative instruments are _____ s which derive their value from the value and characteristics of one or more underlying assets. They can be divided into exchange-traded derivatives and over-the-counter (OTC) derivatives.

Alternatively, _____s can be categorized by 'asset class' depending on whether they are equity based (reflecting ownership of the issuing entity) or debt based (reflecting a loan the investor has made to the issuing entity.) If it is debt, it can be further categorised into short term (less than one year) or long term.

Foreign Exchange instruments and transactions are neither debt nor equity based and belong in their own category.

a. Financial instruments
b. Financial instrument
c. Mark-to-market
d. Market price

25. _____ are cash, evidence of an ownership interest in an entity, or a contractual right to receive, or deliver, cash or another financial instrument.

_____ can be categorized by form depending on whether they are cash instruments or derivative instruments:

- Cash instruments are _____ whose value is determined directly by markets. They can be divided into securities, which are readily transferable, and other cash instruments such as loans and deposits, where both borrower and lender have to agree on a transfer.
- Derivative instruments are _____ which derive their value from the value and characteristics of one or more underlying assets. They can be divided into exchange-traded derivatives and over-the-counter (OTC) derivatives.

Alternatively, _____ can be categorized by 'asset class' depending on whether they are equity based (reflecting ownership of the issuing entity) or debt based (reflecting a loan the investor has made to the issuing entity.) If it is debt, it can be further categorised into short term (less than one year) or long term.

Foreign Exchange instruments and transactions are neither debt nor equity based and belong in their own category.

a. Market liquidity
b. Financial instruments
c. Transfer agent
d. Spot rate

26. The _____ is the former authoritative body of the American Institute of Certified Public Accountants (AICPA.) It was created by the American Institute of Certified Public Accountants in 1959 and issued pronouncements on accounting principles until 1973, when it was replaced by the Financial Accounting Standards Board (FASB.)

Chapter 1. Introduction

The _____ was disbanded in the hopes that the smaller, fully-independent FASB could more effectively create accounting standards.

a. American Payroll Association
b. Institute of Management Accountants
c. International Federation of Accountants
d. Accounting Principles Board

27. _____ were documents issued by the Committee on Accounting Procedure between 1938 and 1959 on various accounting problems. They were discontinued with the dissolution of the Committee in 1959 under a recommendation from the Special Committee on Research Program. In all, 51 bulletins were issued, however, the lack of binding authority over AICPA's membership reduced the influence of, and compliance with the content of the bulletins.

a. Other postemployment benefits
b. AIG
c. Accounting Research Bulletins
d. ABC Television Network

28. The _____ was a predecessor of the Accounting Principles Board, itself a predecessor to the Financial Accounting Standards Board in the United States. Its formation and activities were early efforts to rationalize and legitimize the reporting of business performance. However, it is widely regarded as having failed.

a. Committee on Accounting Procedure
b. Lump sum
c. Price variance
d. Consolidated financial statements

29. _____ is the term used to refer to the standard framework of guidelines for financial accounting used in any given jurisdiction. _____ includes the standards, conventions, and rules accountants follow in recording and summarizing transactions, and in the preparation of financial statements.

Financial accounting information must be assembled and reported objectively.

a. Generally accepted accounting principles
b. Current asset
c. General ledger
d. Long-term liabilities

Chapter 1. Introduction

30. The _____ is located in Norwalk, Connecticut. It is an independent, organization in the private sector that is responsible for oversight of the Financial Accounting Standards Board (FASB), the Governmental Accounting Standards Board (GASB), and their respective advisory councils.

   a. BNSF Railway
   b. 3M Company
   c. BMC Software, Inc.
   d. Financial Accounting Foundation

31. _____ is a term used in accounting, economics and finance to spread the cost of an asset over the span of several years.

In simple words we can say that _____ is the reduction in the value of an asset due to usage, passage of time, wear and tear, technological outdating or obsolescence, depletion, inadequacy, rot, rust, decay or other such factors.

In accounting, _____ is a term used to describe any method of attributing the historical or purchase cost of an asset across its useful life, roughly corresponding to normal wear and tear.

   a. Net profit
   b. Current asset
   c. General ledger
   d. Depreciation

32. _____ LLP, based in Chicago, was once one of the 'Big Five' accounting firms among PricewaterhouseCoopers, Deloitte Touche Tohmatsu, Ernst ' Young and KPMG, providing auditing, tax, and consulting services to large corporations. In 2002, the firm voluntarily surrendered its licenses to practice as Certified Public Accountants in the United States after being found guilty of criminal charges relating to the firm's handling of the auditing of Enron, the energy corporation, resulting in the loss of 85,000 jobs. Although the verdict was subsequently overturned by the Supreme Court of the United States, it has not returned as a viable business.

   a. AIG
   b. Arthur Andersen
   c. AMEX
   d. ABC Television Network

33. _____ is the collection, transport, processing, recycling or disposal, and monitoring of waste materials. The term usually relates to materials produced by human activity, and is generally undertaken to reduce their effect on health, the environment or aesthetics. _____ is also carried out to recover resources from it.

a. BNSF Railway
b. 3M Company
c. Waste Management
d. BMC Software, Inc.

34. _____ is an open standard which supports information modeling and the expression of semantic meaning commonly required in business reporting. _____ is XML-based. It uses the XML syntax and related XML technologies such as XML Schema, XLink, XPath, and Namespaces to articulate this semantic meaning. One use of _____ is to define and exchange financial information, such as a financial statement.
   a. 3M Company
   b. BNSF Railway
   c. BMC Software, Inc.
   d. XBRL

35. _____ are defined as identifiable non-monetary assets that cannot be seen, touched or physically measured, which are created through time and/or effort and that are identifiable as a separate asset. There are two primary forms of intangibles - legal intangibles (such as trade secrets (e.g., customer lists), copyrights, patents, trademarks, and goodwill) and competitive intangibles (such as knowledge activities (know-how, knowledge), collaboration activities, leverage activities, and structural activities.) Legal intangibles are known under the generic term intellectual property and generate legal property rights defensible in a court of law.
   a. Overhead
   b. ABC Television Network
   c. AIG
   d. Intangible assets

36. In law, tangibility is the attribute of being detectable with the senses.

In criminal law, one of the elements of an offense of larceny is that the stolen property must be _____.

In the context of intellectual property, expression in _____ form is one of the requirements for copyright protection.

   a. Nonacquiescence
   b. Tangible
   c. Headnote
   d. Contingent liabilities

Chapter 1. Introduction

37. _____ is a strategic management responsibility that integrates finance, communication, marketing and securities law compliance to enable the most effective two-way communication between a company, the financial community, and other constituencies, which ultimately contributes to a company's securities achieving fair valuation. The term describes the department of a company devoted to handling inquiries from shareholders and investors, as well as others who might be interested in a company's stock or financial stability.

    a. AMEX
    b. Investor Relations
    c. ABC Television Network
    d. AIG

38. _____ is a specific term used in companies' financial reporting from the company-whole point of view. Because that use excludes the effects of changing ownership interest, an economic measure of _____ is necessary for financial analysis from the shareholders' point of view

    _____ is defined by the Financial Accounting Standards Board, or FASB, as 'the change in equity [net assets] of a business enterprise during a period from transactions and other events and circumstances from nonowner sources. It includes all changes in equity during a period except those resulting from investments by owners and distributions to owners.'

    _____ is the sum of net income and other items that must bypass the income statement because they have not been realized, including items like an unrealized holding gain or loss from available for sale securities and foreign currency translation gains or losses.

    a. BNSF Railway
    b. Comprehensive income
    c. 3M Company
    d. BMC Software, Inc.

39. The _____ of 2002 (Pub.L. 107-204, 116 Stat. 745, enacted July 30, 2002), also known as the Public Company Accounting Reform and Investor Protection Act of 2002, is a United States federal law enacted on July 30, 2002 in response to a number of major corporate and accounting scandals including those affecting Enron, Tyco International, Adelphia, Peregrine Systems and WorldCom. The legislation establishes new or enhanced standards for all U.S. public company boards, management, and public accounting firms. It does not apply to privately held companies.

    a. Sarbanes-Oxley Act
    b. Lease
    c. Fair Labor Standards Act
    d. FCPA

Chapter 1. Introduction

40. The _____ was a worldwide economic downturn starting in most places in 1929 and ending at different times in the 1930s or early 1940s for different countries. It was the largest and most important economic depression in the 20th century, and is used in the 21st century as an example of how far the world's economy can fall. The _____ originated in the United States; historians most often use as a starting date the stock market crash on October 29, 1929, known as Black Tuesday.
   a. Great Depression
   b. 3M Company
   c. BNSF Railway
   d. BMC Software, Inc.

41. An _____ is a company whose main business is holding securities of other companies purely for investment purposes. The _____ invests money on behalf of its shareholders who in turn share in the profits and losses.

In United States securities law, there are at least three types of investment companies :

- Open-End Management Investment Companies (mutual funds)
- Closed-End Management Investment Companies (closed-end funds)
- UITs (unit investment trusts)

A fourth and lesser-known type of _____ under the _____ Act of 1940 is a Face-Amount Certificate Company.

   a. AIG
   b. Investment Company
   c. AMEX
   d. ABC Television Network

42. The _____ is an act of Congress. It was passed as a United States Public Law (PL-768) on August 22, 1940, and is codified at 15 U.S.C. § 80a-1 through 15 U.S.C.
   a. Investment Company Act of 1940
   b. ABC Television Network
   c. AMEX
   d. AIG

43. An _____ is the buying of one company by another. An _____ may be friendly or hostile. In the former case, the companies cooperate in negotiations; in the latter case, the takeover target is unwilling to be bought or the target's board has no prior knowledge of the offer. _____ usually refers to a purchase of a smaller firm by a larger one. Sometimes, however, a smaller firm will acquire management control of a larger or longer established company and keep its name for the combined entity. This is known as a reverse takeover.

a. AMEX
b. AIG
c. ABC Television Network
d. Acquisition

44. In business or economics a _____ is a combination of two companies into one larger company. Such actions are commonly voluntary and involve stock swap or cash payment to the target. Stock swap is often used as it allows the shareholders of the two companies to share the risk involved in the deal. A _____ can resemble a takeover but result in a new company name (often combining the names of the original companies) and in new branding; in some cases, terming the combination a '_____' rather than an acquisition is done purely for political or marketing reasons.
   a. 3M Company
   b. Merger
   c. BMC Software, Inc.
   d. BNSF Railway

45. The phrase _____ refers to the aspect of corporate strategy, corporate finance and management dealing with the buying, selling and combining of different companies that can aid, finance, or help a growing company in a given industry grow rapidly without having to create another business entity.
   a. Mergers and acquisitions
   b. BNSF Railway
   c. BMC Software, Inc.
   d. 3M Company

46. A _____ or transnational corporation (TNC) is a corporation or enterprise that manages production or delivers services in more than one country. It can also be referred to as an international corporation. The first modern _____ is generally thought to be the British East India Company, established in 1600.
   a. Butterfield Bank
   b. MicroStrategy
   c. Multinational corporation
   d. Privately held

Chapter 2. Criteria

1. The _____ is a private, not-for-profit organization whose primary purpose is to develop generally accepted accounting principles (GAAP) within the United States in the public's interest. The Securities and Exchange Commission (SEC) designated the _____ as the organization responsible for setting accounting standards for public companies in the U.S. It was created in 1973, replacing the Accounting Principles Board and the Committee on Accounting Procedure of the American Institute of Certified Public Accountants. The _____'s mission is 'to establish and improve standards of financial accounting and reporting for the guidance and education of the public, including issuers, auditors, and users of financial information.'

The _____ is not a governmental body.

   a. Fannie Mae
   b. Financial Accounting Standards Board
   c. Governmental Accounting Standards Board
   d. Public company

2. In accounting, _____ has a very specific meaning. It is an outflow of cash or other valuable assets from a person or company to another person or company. This outflow of cash is generally one side of a trade for products or services that have equal or better current or future value to the buyer than to the seller.

   a. Expense
   b. AMEX
   c. ABC Television Network
   d. AIG

3. In economics, a _____ is a mechanism that allows people to easily buy and sell (trade) financial securities (such as stocks and bonds), commodities (such as precious metals or agricultural goods), and other fungible items of value at low transaction costs and at prices that reflect the efficient-market hypothesis.

They have evolved significantly over several hundred years and are undergoing constant innovation to improve liquidity.

Both general markets (where many commodities are traded) and specialized markets (where only one commodity is traded) exist.

   a. Transfer agent
   b. Spot rate
   c. Mark-to-market
   d. Financial Market

Chapter 2. Criteria

4. A _____ is any one of a variety of different systems, institutions, procedures, social relations and infrastructures whereby persons trade, and goods and services are exchanged, forming part of the economy. It is an arrangement that allows buyers and sellers to exchange things. _____s vary in size, range, geographic scale, location, types and variety of human communities, as well as the types of goods and services traded.

   a. Perfect competition
   b. Market Failure
   c. Market
   d. Recession

5. _____, the Electronic Data-Gathering, Analysis, and Retrieval system, performs automated collection, validation, indexing, acceptance, and forwarding of submissions by companies and others who are required by law to file forms with the U.S. Securities and Exchange Commission (the 'SEC'.) The database is freely available to the public via Web or FTP, typically posting in excess of 3,000 filings per day.

   Not all SEC filings by public companies are available on _____.

   a. AMEX
   b. AIG
   c. ABC Television Network
   d. EDGAR

6. The _____ founded on April 1, 2001 is the successor of the International Accounting Standards Committee (IASC) founded in June 1973 in London. It is responsible for developing the International Financial Reporting Standards (new name for the International Accounting Standards issued after 2001), and promoting the use and application of these standards.

   The _____ is an independent, privately-funded accounting standard-setter based in London, UK.

   a. Emerging technologies
   b. Institute of Management Accountants
   c. Information Systems Audit and Control Association
   d. International Accounting Standards Board

7. _____ is a strategic management responsibility that integrates finance, communication, marketing and securities law compliance to enable the most effective two-way communication between a company, the financial community, and other constituencies, which ultimately contributes to a company's securities achieving fair valuation. The term describes the department of a company devoted to handling inquiries from shareholders and investors, as well as others who might be interested in a company's stock or financial stability.

a. Investor Relations
b. ABC Television Network
c. AMEX
d. AIG

8. _____ is a specific term used in companies' financial reporting from the company-whole point of view. Because that use excludes the effects of changing ownership interest, an economic measure of _____ is necessary for financial analysis from the shareholders' point of view

_____ is defined by the Financial Accounting Standards Board, or FASB, as 'the change in equity [net assets] of a business enterprise during a period from transactions and other events and circumstances from nonowner sources. It includes all changes in equity during a period except those resulting from investments by owners and distributions to owners.'

_____ is the sum of net income and other items that must bypass the income statement because they have not been realized, including items like an unrealized holding gain or loss from available for sale securities and foreign currency translation gains or losses.

a. BNSF Railway
b. Comprehensive income
c. 3M Company
d. BMC Software, Inc.

9. _____ is equal to the income that a firm has after subtracting costs and expenses from the total revenue. _____ can be distributed among holders of common stock as a dividend or held by the firm as retained earnings.

The items deducted will typically include tax expense, financing expense (interest expense), and minority interest. Likewise, preferred stock dividends will be subtracted too, though they are not an expense.

a. Matching principle
b. Generally accepted accounting principles
c. Long-term liabilities
d. Net income

10. In business and finance accounting, _____ is equal to the gross profit minus overheads minus interest payable plus/minus one off items for a given time period (usually: accounting period.)

A common synonym for '_____' when discussing financial statements (which include a balance sheet and an income statement) is the bottom line. This term results from the traditional appearance of an income statement which shows all allocated revenues and expenses over a specified time period with the resulting summation on the bottom line of the report.

   a. Cost of goods sold
   b. Salvage value
   c. Treasury stock
   d. Net profit

11. _____ is an open standard which supports information modeling and the expression of semantic meaning commonly required in business reporting. _____ is XML-based. It uses the XML syntax and related XML technologies such as XML Schema, XLink, XPath, and Namespaces to articulate this semantic meaning. One use of _____ is to define and exchange financial information, such as a financial statement.
   a. 3M Company
   b. BNSF Railway
   c. BMC Software, Inc.
   d. XBRL

12. _____ was founded in June 1973 in London and replaced by the International Accounting Standards Board on April 1, 2001. It was responsible for developing the International Accounting Standards and promoting the use and application of these standards.

Chapter 2. Criteria

The _____ was founded as a result of an agreement between accountancy bodies in the following countries:

- Australia (Institute of Chartered Accountants in Australia (ICAA) and the CPA Australia (formerly known as Australian Society of Certified Practising Accountants (ASCPA))

- Canada (Canadian Institute of Chartered Accountants (CICA))

- France (Ordre des Experts Comptable et des Comptables Agrees (Order of Accounting Experts and Qualified Accountants))

- Germany and the Wirtschaftsprüferkammer (WPK) (Chamber of Auditors))

- Japan Nihon Kouninkaikeishi Kyoukai)

- Mexico (Instituto Mexicano de Contadores Publicos (IMCP) (Mexican Institute of Public Accountants)) (removed from the board in 1987 due to non-payment of dues; resumed in 1995.)

- the Netherlands (Nederlands Instituut van Registeraccountants (NIVRA)

(Netherlands Institute of Registered Auditors))

- the United Kingdom and Ireland (counted as one) (Institute of Chartered Accountants in England and Wales (ICAEW), Institute of Chartered Accountants of Scotland (ICAS), Institute of Chartered Accountants in Ireland (ICAI), Association of Certified Accountants, Institute of Cost and Management Accountants, and the Institute of Municipal Treasurers and Accountants)

- the United States of America (American Institute of Certified Public Accountants (AICPA))

The Institute of Chartered Accountants of Nigeria became an associate member in 1976 and a member of the board from 1978 to 1987.

The National Council of Chartered Accountants (South Africa) became an associate member in 1974 and joined the board in 1978.

a. International Accounting Standards Committee
b. International Accounting Standards Board
c. American Accounting Association
d. American Payroll Association

Chapter 2. Criteria

13. _____, also called fair price (in a commonplace conflation of the two distinct concepts), is a concept used in finance and economics, defined as a rational and unbiased estimate of the potential market price of a good, service, or asset, taking into account such objective factors as:

- acquisition/production/distribution costs, replacement costs, or costs of close substitutes
- actual utility at a given level of development of social productive capability
- supply vs. demand

and subjective factors such as

- risk characteristics
- cost of capital
- individually perceived utility

In accounting, _____ is used as an estimate of the market value of an asset (or liability) for which a market price cannot be determined (usually because there is no established market for the asset.) Under GAAP (FAS 157), _____ is the amount at which the asset could be bought or sold in a current transaction between willing parties, or transferred to an equivalent party, other than in a liquidation sale. This is used for assets whose carrying value is based on mark-to-market valuations; for assets carried at historical cost, the _____ of the asset is not used. One example of where _____ is an issue is a College kitchen with a cost of $2 million which was built 5 years ago.

a. BMC Software, Inc.
b. BNSF Railway
c. Fair value
d. 3M Company

14. The _____ of 2002 (Pub.L. 107-204, 116 Stat. 745, enacted July 30, 2002), also known as the Public Company Accounting Reform and Investor Protection Act of 2002, is a United States federal law enacted on July 30, 2002 in response to a number of major corporate and accounting scandals including those affecting Enron, Tyco International, Adelphia, Peregrine Systems and WorldCom. The legislation establishes new or enhanced standards for all U.S. public company boards, management, and public accounting firms. It does not apply to privately held companies.

a. FCPA
b. Sarbanes-Oxley Act
c. Fair Labor Standards Act
d. Lease

15. A _____ is a fungible, negotiable instrument representing financial value. they are broadly categorized into debt securities (such as banknotes, bonds and debentures), and equity securities; e.g., common stocks. The company or other entity issuing the _____ is called the issuer.

a. Tracking stock
b. Security
c. 3M Company
d. BMC Software, Inc.

16. The U.S. _____ is an independent agency of the United States government which holds primary responsibility for enforcing the federal securities laws and regulating the securities industry, the nation's stock and options exchanges, and other electronic securities markets. The SEC was created by section 4 of the Securities Exchange Act of 1934 (now codified as 15 U.S.C. ÂÂ§ 78d and commonly referred to as the 1934 Act.)
a. Securities and Exchange Commission
b. BNSF Railway
c. BMC Software, Inc.
d. 3M Company

17. An _____ is a practitioner of accountancy, which is the measurement, disclosure or provision of assurance about financial information that helps managers, investors, tax authorities and other decision makers make resource allocation decisions.

The word '_____' is derived from the French 'Compter' which took its origin from the Latin 'Computare'. The word was formerly written in English as 'Accomptant', but in process of time the word, which was always pronounced by dropping the 'p', became gradually changed both in pronunciation and in orthography to its present form.

a. AIG
b. ABC Television Network
c. AMEX
d. Accountant

18. The _____ is the national, professional association of CPAs in the United States, with more than 330,000 members, including CPAs in business and industry, public practice, government, and education; student affiliates; and international associates. It sets ethical standards for the profession and U.S. auditing standards for audits of private companies; federal, state and local governments; and non-profit organizations.

Approximately 40% of its members are engaged in the practice of public accounting, in areas such as auditing, accounting, taxation, general business consulting, business valuation, personal financial planning and business technology.

Chapter 2. Criteria

a. AIG
b. American Institute of Certified Public Accountants
c. ABC Television Network
d. Other postemployment benefits

19. _____ is the statutory title of qualified accountants in the United States who have passed the Uniform _____ Examination and have met additional state education and experience requirements for certification as a _____. Individuals who have passed the Exam but have not either accomplished the required on-the-job experience or have previously met it but in the meantime have lapsed their continuing professional education are, in many states, permitted the designation '_____ Inactive' or an equivalent phrase. In most U.S. states, only _____s who are licensed are able to provide to the public attestation (including auditing) opinions on financial statements.

a. Certified Public Accountant
b. Certified General Accountant
c. Chartered Accountant
d. Chartered Certified Accountant

20. A _____ or transnational corporation (TNC) is a corporation or enterprise that manages production or delivers services in more than one country. It can also be referred to as an international corporation. The first modern _____ is generally thought to be the British East India Company, established in 1600.

a. Privately held
b. Butterfield Bank
c. MicroStrategy
d. Multinational corporation

21. The general definition of an _____ is an evaluation of a person, organization, system, process, project or product. _____s are performed to ascertain the validity and reliability of information; also to provide an assessment of a system's internal control. The goal of an _____ is to express an opinion on the person/organization/system (etc) in question, under evaluation based on work done on a test basis.

a. Institute of Chartered Accountants of India
b. Audit regime
c. Assurance service
d. Audit

22. _____ is the term used to refer to the standard framework of guidelines for financial accounting used in any given jurisdiction. _____ includes the standards, conventions, and rules accountants follow in recording and summarizing transactions, and in the preparation of financial statements.

Financial accounting information must be assembled and reported objectively.

a. Current asset
b. Long-term liabilities
c. Generally accepted accounting principles
d. General ledger

23. In business and accounting, _____ are everything of value that is owned by a person or company. It is a claim on the property your income of a borrower. The balance sheet of a firm records the monetary value of the _____ owned by the firm.

a. Accrual basis accounting
b. Accounts receivable
c. Assets
d. Earnings before interest, taxes, depreciation and amortization

24. _____ and credit are formal bookkeeping and accounting terms. They are the most fundamental concepts in accounting, representing the two records that one party in a transaction makes on its records, transferring a money balance from one account to another, one representing a reduction of liability or increase in asset, and the other representing a balancing increase in liability or reduction of asset.

Introduction

_____s and credits are a system of notation used in accounting to keep track of money movements (transactions) into and out of an account.

a. Debit and credit
b. Debit
c. Cookie jar accounting
d. Bookkeeping

25. In financial accounting, a _____ is defined as an obligation of an entity arising from past transactions or events, the settlement of which may result in the transfer or use of assets, provision of services or other yielding of economic benefits in the future.

a. False Claims Act
b. Liability
c. Corporate governance
d. Vested

Chapter 2. Criteria

26. In financial accounting, a _____ or statement of financial position is a summary of a person's or organization's balances. Assets, liabilities and ownership equity are listed as of a specific date, such as the end of its financial year. A _____ is often described as a snapshot of a company's financial condition.
    a. Statement of retained earnings
    b. 3M Company
    c. Financial statements
    d. Balance sheet

27. _____ are formal records of a business' financial activities.

    In British English, including United Kingdom company law, _____ are often referred to as accounts, although the term _____ is also used, particularly by accountants.

    _____ provide an overview of a business' financial condition in both short and long term.

    a. 3M Company
    b. Statement of retained earnings
    c. Financial statements
    d. Notes to the financial statements

28. _____ is a company's financial statement that indicates how the revenue is transformed into the net income The purpose of the _____ is to show managers and investors whether the company made or lost money during the period being reported.

    The important thing to remember about an _____ is that it represents a period of time.

    a. ABC Television Network
    b. AIG
    c. Income statement
    d. AMEX

29. The _____ is currently the source of generally accepted accounting principles (GAAP) used by State and Local governments in the [[United States of America]]. As with most of the entities involved in creating GAAP in the United States, it is a private, non-governmental organization.

    The _____ is subject to oversight by the Financial Accounting Foundation (FAF), which selects the members of the _____ and the Financial Accounting Standards Board, and funds both organizations.

a. Multinational corporation
b. Fannie Mae
c. National Conference of Commissioners on Uniform State Laws
d. Governmental Accounting Standards Board

30. _____ is the balance of the amounts of cash being received and paid by a business during a defined period of time, sometimes tied to a specific project. Measurement of _____ can be used

- to evaluate the state or performance of a business or project.
- to determine problems with liquidity. Being profitable does not necessarily mean being liquid. A company can fail because of a shortage of cash, even while profitable.
- to project rate of returns. The time of _____s into and out of projects are used as inputs to financial models such as internal rate of return, and net present value.
- to examine income or growth of a business when it is believed that accrual accounting concepts do not represent economic realities. Alternately, _____ can be used to 'validate' the net income generated by accrual accounting.

_____ as a generic term may be used differently depending on context, and certain _____ definitions may be adapted by analysts and users for their own uses. Common terms include operating _____ and free _____.

a. Controlling interest
b. Flow-through entity
c. Commercial paper
d. Cash flow

31. In financial accounting, a _____ or Statement of cash flows is a financial statement that shows a company's flow of cash. The money coming into the business is called cash inflow, and money going out from the business is called cash outflow. The statement shows how changes in balance sheet and income accounts affect cash and cash equivalents, and breaks the analysis down to operating, investing, and financing activities.
a. BMC Software, Inc.
b. Cash flow statement
c. 3M Company
d. BNSF Railway

32. _____ are financial statements that factor the holding company's subsidiaries into its aggregated accounting figure. It is a representation of how the holding company is doing as a group. The consolidated accounts should provide a true and fair view of the financial and operating conditions of the group.

a. Replacement cost
b. Committee on Accounting Procedure
c. Consolidated financial statements
d. Redemption value

33. _____ is a term used in accounting, economics and finance to spread the cost of an asset over the span of several years.

In simple words we can say that _____ is the reduction in the value of an asset due to usage, passage of time, wear and tear, technological outdating or obsolescence, depletion, inadequacy, rot, rust, decay or other such factors.

In accounting, _____ is a term used to describe any method of attributing the historical or purchase cost of an asset across its useful life, roughly corresponding to normal wear and tear.

a. Net profit
b. Depreciation
c. Current asset
d. General ledger

34. _____ is a political and social term from the Latin verb conservare meaning to save or preserve. As the name suggests it usually indicates support for tradition and traditional values though the meaning has changed in different countries and time periods. The modern political term conservative was used by French politician Chateaubriand in 1819.

a. Conservatism
b. 3M Company
c. BMC Software, Inc.
d. Politicized issue

35. A _____ is a business that functions without the intention or threat of liquidation for the foreseeable future, usually regarded as at least within 12 months.

In accounting, '_____' refers to a company's ability to continue functioning as a business entity. It is the responsibility of the directors to assess whether the _____ assumption is appropriate when preparing the financial statements.

a. Payment
b. 3M Company
c. Going concern
d. BMC Software, Inc.

Chapter 3. The Financial Position Statement

1. In financial accounting, a _____ or statement of financial position is a summary of a person's or organization's balances. Assets, liabilities and ownership equity are listed as of a specific date, such as the end of its financial year. A _____ is often described as a snapshot of a company's financial condition.
    a. Financial statements
    b. 3M Company
    c. Statement of retained earnings
    d. Balance sheet

2. _____ is an open standard which supports information modeling and the expression of semantic meaning commonly required in business reporting. _____ is XML-based. It uses the XML syntax and related XML technologies such as XML Schema, XLink, XPath, and Namespaces to articulate this semantic meaning. One use of _____ is to define and exchange financial information, such as a financial statement.
    a. 3M Company
    b. BNSF Railway
    c. BMC Software, Inc.
    d. XBRL

3. In business and accounting, _____ are everything of value that is owned by a person or company. It is a claim on the property your income of a borrower. The balance sheet of a firm records the monetary value of the _____ owned by the firm.
    a. Accounts receivable
    b. Earnings before interest, taxes, depreciation and amortization
    c. Accrual basis accounting
    d. Assets

4. _____ and credit are formal bookkeeping and accounting terms. They are the most fundamental concepts in accounting, representing the two records that one party in a transaction makes on its records, transferring a money balance from one account to another, one representing a reduction of liability or increase in asset, and the other representing a balancing increase in liability or reduction of asset.

Introduction

_____s and credits are a system of notation used in accounting to keep track of money movements (transactions) into and out of an account.

   a. Debit and credit
   b. Cookie jar accounting
   c. Bookkeeping
   d. Debit

Chapter 3. The Financial Position Statement

5. _____, also called fair price (in a commonplace conflation of the two distinct concepts), is a concept used in finance and economics, defined as a rational and unbiased estimate of the potential market price of a good, service, or asset, taking into account such objective factors as:

- acquisition/production/distribution costs, replacement costs, or costs of close substitutes
- actual utility at a given level of development of social productive capability
- supply vs. demand

and subjective factors such as

- risk characteristics
- cost of capital
- individually perceived utility

In accounting, _____ is used as an estimate of the market value of an asset (or liability) for which a market price cannot be determined (usually because there is no established market for the asset.) Under GAAP (FAS 157), _____ is the amount at which the asset could be bought or sold in a current transaction between willing parties, or transferred to an equivalent party, other than in a liquidation sale. This is used for assets whose carrying value is based on mark-to-market valuations; for assets carried at historical cost, the _____ of the asset is not used. One example of where _____ is an issue is a College kitchen with a cost of $2 million which was built 5 years ago.

a. 3M Company
b. BNSF Railway
c. BMC Software, Inc.
d. Fair value

6. In financial accounting, a _____ is defined as an obligation of an entity arising from past transactions or events, the settlement of which may result in the transfer or use of assets, provision of services or other yielding of economic benefits in the future.
a. False Claims Act
b. Corporate governance
c. Vested
d. Liability

7. In finance, or business _____ is the ability of an entity to pay its debts with available cash. _____ can also be described as the ability of a corporation to meet its long-term fixed expenses and to accomplish long-term expansion and growth. The better a company's _____, the better it is financially.

Chapter 3. The Financial Position Statement

   a. Capital asset
   b. BMC Software, Inc.
   c. Solvency
   d. 3M Company

8. The term '_____' refers to the concept of collecting information and attempting to spot a pattern in the information. In some fields of study, the term '_____' has more formally-defined meanings.

In project management _____ is a mathematical technique that uses historical results to predict future outcome.

   a. 3M Company
   b. Multicollinearity
   c. Regression analysis
   d. Trend analysis

9. _____ of something is, in finance, the adding together of interest or different investments over a period of time such as atoms (1 - the act or process of accruing; 2 - the amount that accrues.) It holds specific meanings in accounting and payroll.

_____, in accounting, describes the accounting method known as _____ basis, whereby revenues and expenses are recognized when they are accrued, i.e. accumulated (earned or incurred), regardless when the actual cash is received or paid out.

   a. Earnings before interest, taxes, depreciation and amortization
   b. Accrual
   c. Assets
   d. Accounts receivable

10. _____ is a method of accounting whereby economic activities (rather than cash flow) of financial events are considered, because of two complementary principles, which (together) determine the point, at which expenses and revenues are recognized. According to revenue recognition principle, revenues are realized when earned, whether or not they are received in cash.
   a. Accrued revenue
   b. Accrual
   c. Earnings before interest, taxes, depreciation and amortization
   d. Accrual basis accounting

Chapter 3. The Financial Position Statement

11. _____ is a term used in accounting, economics and finance to spread the cost of an asset over the span of several years.

In simple words we can say that _____ is the reduction in the value of an asset due to usage, passage of time, wear and tear, technological outdating or obsolescence, depletion, inadequacy, rot, rust, decay or other such factors.

In accounting, _____ is a term used to describe any method of attributing the historical or purchase cost of an asset across its useful life, roughly corresponding to normal wear and tear.

a. General ledger
b. Current asset
c. Depreciation
d. Net profit

12. The _____ is a 'voluntary organization of persons interested in accounting education and research'. It was formed in 1916. Its main publication, the The Accounting Review, was first published in 1926.
a. Australian Accounting Standards Board
b. Institute of Management Accountants
c. International Accounting Standards Board
d. American Accounting Association

13. In economics, a _____ is a mechanism that allows people to easily buy and sell (trade) financial securities (such as stocks and bonds), commodities (such as precious metals or agricultural goods), and other fungible items of value at low transaction costs and at prices that reflect the efficient-market hypothesis.

They have evolved significantly over several hundred years and are undergoing constant innovation to improve liquidity.

Both general markets (where many commodities are traded) and specialized markets (where only one commodity is traded) exist.

a. Spot rate
b. Financial Market
c. Transfer agent
d. Mark-to-market

Chapter 3. The Financial Position Statement

14. A _____ is any one of a variety of different systems, institutions, procedures, social relations and infrastructures whereby persons trade, and goods and services are exchanged, forming part of the economy. It is an arrangement that allows buyers and sellers to exchange things. _____s vary in size, range, geographic scale, location, types and variety of human communities, as well as the types of goods and services traded.
   a. Perfect competition
   b. Market Failure
   c. Recession
   d. Market

15. A _____ is a fungible, negotiable instrument representing financial value. they are broadly categorized into debt securities (such as banknotes, bonds and debentures), and equity securities; e.g., common stocks. The company or other entity issuing the _____ is called the issuer.
   a. 3M Company
   b. Security
   c. Tracking stock
   d. BMC Software, Inc.

16. The U.S. _____ is an independent agency of the United States government which holds primary responsibility for enforcing the federal securities laws and regulating the securities industry, the nation's stock and options exchanges, and other electronic securities markets. The SEC was created by section 4 of the Securities Exchange Act of 1934 (now codified as 15 U.S.C. §Â§ 78d and commonly referred to as the 1934 Act.)
   a. Securities and Exchange Commission
   b. BMC Software, Inc.
   c. 3M Company
   d. BNSF Railway

17. _____, in accrual accounting, is any account where the asset or liability is not realized until a future date (accounting period), e.g. annuities, charges, taxes, income, etc. The _____ item may be carried, dependent on type of deferral, as either an asset or liability.
   a. Pro forma
   b. Payroll
   c. Deferred
   d. Cash basis accounting

18. _____, in accrual accounting, (e.g. advance payment received from a client) is, according to revenue recognition, revenue not earned until the delivery of goods or services, which until then, is still owed to the payer, hence remaining a liability.

_____, sometimes referred to as deferred revenue or unearned revenue, shares characteristics with accrued expense with the difference that a liability to be covered latter is cash received FROM a counterpart, while goods or services are to be delivered in a latter period, when such income item is earned, the related revenue item is recognized, and the same amount is deducted from deferred revenues.

a. Deferred income
b. Matching principle
c. Gross sales
d. Treasury stock

19. In accounting, _____ has a very specific meaning. It is an outflow of cash or other valuable assets from a person or company to another person or company. This outflow of cash is generally one side of a trade for products or services that have equal or better current or future value to the buyer than to the seller.

a. Expense
b. ABC Television Network
c. AMEX
d. AIG

20. An _____ is a tax levied on the financial income of people, corporations, or other legal entities. Various _____ systems exist, with varying degrees of tax incidence. Income taxation can be progressive, proportional, or regressive.

a. Individual Retirement Arrangement
b. Income tax
c. Implied level of government service
d. Ordinary income

21. _____ is generally understood in financial circles as the point at which revenue is recognized, typically through a transaction which involves the exchange of an asset, product, or service for cash or its equivalents.

This approach gives the accounting division a strictly objective basis for changing the books. For example, a homeowner may believe that his house has grown in value during a strong market, or fallen in value during a weak market, but until the house is actually sold for a specific price to a specific buyer, the change in value can only be estimated and is considered unrealized.

a. Total-factor productivity
b. Realization
c. Valuation
d. Merck ' Co., Inc.

22. The _____ is a private, not-for-profit organization whose primary purpose is to develop generally accepted accounting principles (GAAP) within the United States in the public's interest. The Securities and Exchange Commission (SEC) designated the _____ as the organization responsible for setting accounting standards for public companies in the U.S. It was created in 1973, replacing the Accounting Principles Board and the Committee on Accounting Procedure of the American Institute of Certified Public Accountants. The _____'s mission is 'to establish and improve standards of financial accounting and reporting for the guidance and education of the public, including issuers, auditors, and users of financial information.'

The _____ is not a governmental body.

a. Governmental Accounting Standards Board
b. Public company
c. Financial Accounting Standards Board
d. Fannie Mae

23. In economics, _____ or _____ goods or real _____ refers to factors of production used to create goods or services that are not themselves significantly consumed (though they may depreciate) in the production process. _____ goods may be acquired with money or financial _____. In finance and accounting, _____ generally refers to financial wealth, especially that used to start or maintain a business.
a. Screening
b. Vyborg Appeal
c. Capital
d. Disclosure

24. In economics, business, retail, and accounting, a _____ is the value of money that has been used up to produce something, and hence is not available for use anymore. In economics, a _____ is an alternative that is given up as a result of a decision. In business, the _____ may be one of acquisition, in which case the amount of money expended to acquire it is counted as _____.
a. Prime cost
b. Cost
c. Cost allocation
d. Cost of quality

25. _____ is the term used to refer to the standard framework of guidelines for financial accounting used in any given jurisdiction. _____ includes the standards, conventions, and rules accountants follow in recording and summarizing transactions, and in the preparation of financial statements.

Financial accounting information must be assembled and reported objectively.

a. Current asset
b. Long-term liabilities
c. General ledger
d. Generally accepted accounting principles

26. The term _____ or replacement value refers to the amount that an entity would have to pay, at the present time, to replace any one of its assets.

In the insurance industry, '_____' is a method of computing the value of an item insured. _____ is not market value, but is instead the cost to replace an item or structure at its pre-loss condition.

a. Replacement cost
b. Consolidated financial statements
c. Time and motion study
d. Channel stuffing

27. _____ is the balance of the amounts of cash being received and paid by a business during a defined period of time, sometimes tied to a specific project. Measurement of _____ can be used

- to evaluate the state or performance of a business or project.
- to determine problems with liquidity. Being profitable does not necessarily mean being liquid. A company can fail because of a shortage of cash, even while profitable.
- to project rate of returns. The time of _____s into and out of projects are used as inputs to financial models such as internal rate of return, and net present value.
- to examine income or growth of a business when it is believed that accrual accounting concepts do not represent economic realities. Alternately, _____ can be used to 'validate' the net income generated by accrual accounting.

_____ as a generic term may be used differently depending on context, and certain _____ definitions may be adapted by analysts and users for their own uses. Common terms include operating _____ and free _____.

a. Controlling interest
b. Cash flow
c. Flow-through entity
d. Commercial paper

28. In financial accounting, a _____ or Statement of cash flows is a financial statement that shows a company's flow of cash. The money coming into the business is called cash inflow, and money going out from the business is called cash outflow. The statement shows how changes in balance sheet and income accounts affect cash and cash equivalents, and breaks the analysis down to operating, investing, and financing activities.
   a. Cash flow statement
   b. 3M Company
   c. BNSF Railway
   d. BMC Software, Inc.

29. _____ is a company's financial statement that indicates how the revenue is transformed into the net income The purpose of the _____ is to show managers and investors whether the company made or lost money during the period being reported.

The important thing to remember about an _____ is that it represents a period of time.

   a. AMEX
   b. AIG
   c. Income statement
   d. ABC Television Network

30. The _____ of 2002 (Pub.L. 107-204, 116 Stat. 745, enacted July 30, 2002), also known as the Public Company Accounting Reform and Investor Protection Act of 2002, is a United States federal law enacted on July 30, 2002 in response to a number of major corporate and accounting scandals including those affecting Enron, Tyco International, Adelphia, Peregrine Systems and WorldCom. The legislation establishes new or enhanced standards for all U.S. public company boards, management, and public accounting firms. It does not apply to privately held companies.
   a. Lease
   b. Sarbanes-Oxley Act
   c. Fair Labor Standards Act
   d. FCPA

31. A _____ is a type of debt Like all debt instruments, a _____ entails the redistribution of financial assets over time, between the lender and the borrower.

Chapter 3. The Financial Position Statement

a. Loan
b. Lender
c. Loan to value
d. Debenture

32. _____ is a strategic management responsibility that integrates finance, communication, marketing and securities law compliance to enable the most effective two-way communication between a company, the financial community, and other constituencies, which ultimately contributes to a company's securities achieving fair valuation. The term describes the department of a company devoted to handling inquiries from shareholders and investors, as well as others who might be interested in a company's stock or financial stability.

a. AMEX
b. AIG
c. ABC Television Network
d. Investor Relations

33. In finance, the _____ or quick ratio or liquid ratio measures the ability of a company to use its near cash or quick assets to immediately extinguish or retire its current liabilities. Quick assets include those current assets that presumably can be quickly converted to cash at close to their book values.

$$\text{Quick (Acid Test) Ratio} = \frac{\text{Cash} + \text{Marketable Securities} + \text{Accounts Receivables}}{\text{Current Liabilities}}$$

Generally, the acid test ratio should be 1:1 or better, however this varies widely by industry.

a. Earnings per share
b. Invested capital
c. Acid-Test
d. Inventory turnover

34. In finance, a _____ is a debt security, in which the authorized issuer owes the holders a debt and, depending on the terms of the _____, is obliged to pay interest (the coupon) and/or to repay the principal at a later date, termed maturity. It is a formal contract to repay borrowed money with interest at fixed intervals.

Thus a _____ is like a loan: the issuer is the borrower, the _____ holder is the lender, and the coupon is the interest.

Chapter 3. The Financial Position Statement

a. Revenue bonds
b. Zero-coupon bond
c. Bond
d. Coupon rate

35. _____ is a business, economics or investment term that refers to an asset's ability to be easily converted through an act of buying or selling without causing a significant movement in the price and with minimum loss of value. Money, or cash on hand, is the most liquid asset. An act of exchange of a less liquid asset with a more liquid asset is called liquidation.

a. Spot rate
b. Transfer agent
c. Financial instruments
d. Market liquidity

36. In business, _____ is the total assets minus total outside liabilities of an individual or a company. For a company, this is called shareholders' equity and may be referred to as book value. _____ is stated as at a particular point in time.

a. Creditor
b. Debtor
c. Net worth
d. Restructuring

37. An _____ is a practitioner of accountancy, which is the measurement, disclosure or provision of assurance about financial information that helps managers, investors, tax authorities and other decision makers make resource allocation decisions.

The word '_____' is derived from the French 'Compter' which took its origin from the Latin 'Computare'. The word was formerly written in English as 'Accomptant', but in process of time the word, which was always pronounced by dropping the 'p', became gradually changed both in pronunciation and in orthography to its present form.

a. AIG
b. Accountant
c. ABC Television Network
d. AMEX

38. The _____ is the national, professional association of CPAs in the United States, with more than 330,000 members, including CPAs in business and industry, public practice, government, and education; student affiliates; and international associates. It sets ethical standards for the profession and U.S. auditing standards for audits of private companies; federal, state and local governments; and non-profit organizations.

Chapter 3. The Financial Position Statement 39

Approximately 40% of its members are engaged in the practice of public accounting, in areas such as auditing, accounting, taxation, general business consulting, business valuation, personal financial planning and business technology.

a. ABC Television Network
b. Other postemployment benefits
c. AIG
d. American Institute of Certified Public Accountants

39. _____ is the statutory title of qualified accountants in the United States who have passed the Uniform _____ Examination and have met additional state education and experience requirements for certification as a _____. Individuals who have passed the Exam but have not either accomplished the required on-the-job experience or have previously met it but in the meantime have lapsed their continuing professional education are, in many states, permitted the designation '_____ Inactive' or an equivalent phrase. In most U.S. states, only _____s who are licensed are able to provide to the public attestation (including auditing) opinions on financial statements.

a. Chartered Accountant
b. Certified General Accountant
c. Chartered Certified Accountant
d. Certified Public Accountant

40. _____ is a political and social term from the Latin verb conservare meaning to save or preserve. As the name suggests it usually indicates support for tradition and traditional values though the meaning has changed in different countries and time periods. The modern political term conservative was used by French politician Chateaubriand in 1819.

a. Politicized issue
b. 3M Company
c. BMC Software, Inc.
d. Conservatism

41. In accounting, a _____ is an asset on the balance sheet which is expected to be sold or otherwise used up in the near future, usually within one year, or one business cycle - whichever is longer. Typical _____s include cash, cash equivalents, accounts receivable, inventory, the portion of prepaid accounts which will be used within a year, and short-term investments.

On the balance sheet, assets will typically be classified into _____s and long-term assets.

a. Deferred
b. General ledger
c. Pro forma
d. Current asset

42. A _____ is the pinnacle activity involved in selling products or services in return for money or other compensation. It is an act of completion of a commercial activity.

A _____ is completed by the seller, the owner of the goods.

a. Sale
b. Tertiary sector of economy
c. High yield stock
d. Maturity

43. _____s are cash, evidence of an ownership interest in an entity or deliver, cash or another _____.

_____s can be categorized by form depending on whether they are cash instruments or derivative instruments:

- Cash instruments are _____s whose value is determined directly by markets. They can be divided into securities, which are readily transferable, and other cash instruments such as loans and deposits, where both borrower and lender have to agree on a transfer.
- Derivative instruments are _____s which derive their value from the value and characteristics of one or more underlying assets. They can be divided into exchange-traded derivatives and over-the-counter (OTC) derivatives.

Alternatively, _____s can be categorized by 'asset class' depending on whether they are equity based (reflecting ownership of the issuing entity) or debt based (reflecting a loan the investor has made to the issuing entity.) If it is debt, it can be further categorised into short term (less than one year) or long term.

Foreign Exchange instruments and transactions are neither debt nor equity based and belong in their own category.

a. Financial instrument
b. Financial instruments
c. Mark-to-market
d. Market price

44. _____ are cash, evidence of an ownership interest in an entity, or a contractual right to receive, or deliver, cash or another financial instrument.

_____ can be categorized by form depending on whether they are cash instruments or derivative instruments:

- Cash instruments are _____ whose value is determined directly by markets. They can be divided into securities, which are readily transferable, and other cash instruments such as loans and deposits, where both borrower and lender have to agree on a transfer.
- Derivative instruments are _____ which derive their value from the value and characteristics of one or more underlying assets. They can be divided into exchange-traded derivatives and over-the-counter (OTC) derivatives.

Alternatively, _____ can be categorized by 'asset class' depending on whether they are equity based (reflecting ownership of the issuing entity) or debt based (reflecting a loan the investor has made to the issuing entity.) If it is debt, it can be further categorised into short term (less than one year) or long term.

Foreign Exchange instruments and transactions are neither debt nor equity based and belong in their own category.

a. Transfer agent
b. Spot rate
c. Market liquidity
d. Financial instruments

45. _____ is the planning process used to determine whether a firm's long term investments such as new machinery, replacement machinery, new plants, new products, and research development projects are worth pursuing. It is budget for major capital, or investment, expenditures.

Many formal methods are used in _____, including the techniques such as

- Net present value
- Profitability index
- Internal rate of return
- Modified Internal Rate of Return
- Equivalent annuity

These methods use the incremental cash flows from each potential investment, or project. Techniques based on accounting earnings and accounting rules are sometimes used - though economists consider this to be improper - such as the accounting rate of return, and 'return on investment.' Simplified and hybrid methods are used as well, such as payback period and discounted payback period.

a. Preferred stock
b. Gross profit
c. Cash flow
d. Capital Budgeting

46. _____ is a type of lease - the other being an operating lease. A _____ effectively allows a firm to finance the purchase of an asset, even if, strictly speaking, the firm never acquires the asset. Typically, a _____ will give the lessee control over an asset for a large proportion of the asset's useful life, providing them the benefits and risks of ownership.

a. Finance lease
b. Debt ratio
c. 3M Company
d. Profitability index

47. A _____ is a contract conferring a right on one person to possess property belonging to another person (called a landlord or lessor) to the exclusion of the owner landlord. It is a rental agreement between landlord and tenant. The relationship between the tenant and the landlord is called a tenancy, and the right to possession by the tenant is sometimes called a leasehold interest.

a. Robinson-Patman Act
b. Federal Sentencing Guidelines
c. Model Code of Professional Responsibility
d. Lease

48. _____ refers to income that is not a wage.

It includes interest, dividends or realized capital gains from investments, rent from land or property ownership, and any other income that does not derive from work.

_____ has often been treated differently for tax purposes than earned income, in order to redistribute income or to recognize its qualitative difference from income derived from work.

a. AMEX
b. ABC Television Network
c. AIG
d. Unearned income

49. Project _____: The project _____ is a prediction of the costs associated with a particular company project. These costs include labor, materials, and other related expenses. The project _____ is often broken down into specific tasks, with task _____s assigned to each.

a. BNSF Railway
b. 3M Company
c. Budget
d. BMC Software, Inc.

50. The _____ is a Cabinet-level office, and is the largest office within the Executive Office of the President of the United States (EOP.) It is an important conduit by which the White House oversees the activities of federal agencies. OMB is tasked with giving expert advice to senior White House officials on a range of topics relating to federal policy, management, legislative, regulatory, and budgetary issues.
   a. AT'T Wireless Services, Inc.
   b. Office of Management and Budget
   c. Analysis of variance
   d. Alaska Air Group

51. In finance, a _____ is a type of bond that can be converted into shares of stock in the issuing company, usually at some pre-announced ratio. It is a hybrid security with debt- and equity-like features. Although it typically has a low coupon rate, the holder is compensated with the ability to convert the bond to common stock, usually at a substantial discount to the stock's market value.
   a. Convertible bond
   b. Zero-coupon
   c. Zero-coupon bond
   d. Coupon rate

52. The term _____ or superannuation refers to a pension granted upon retirement. They may be set up by employers, insurance companies, the government or other institutions such as employer associations or trade unions.
   a. Wage
   b. 3M Company
   c. BMC Software, Inc.
   d. Retirement plan

53. _____ are formal records of a business' financial activities.

In British English, including United Kingdom company law, _____ are often referred to as accounts, although the term _____ is also used, particularly by accountants.

_____ provide an overview of a business' financial condition in both short and long term.

Chapter 3. The Financial Position Statement

a. Notes to the financial statements
b. 3M Company
c. Financial statements
d. Statement of retained earnings

54. The general definition of an _____ is an evaluation of a person, organization, system, process, project or product. _____s are performed to ascertain the validity and reliability of information; also to provide an assessment of a system's internal control. The goal of an _____ is to express an opinion on the person/organization/system (etc) in question, under evaluation based on work done on a test basis.
   a. Institute of Chartered Accountants of India
   b. Assurance service
   c. Audit
   d. Audit regime

55. The _____ is a financial ratio that measures whether or not a firm has enough resources to pay its debts over the next 12 months. It compares a firm's current assets to its current liabilities. It is expressed as follows:

$$\text{Current ratio} = \frac{\text{Current Assets}}{\text{Current Liabilities}}$$

For example, if WXY Company's current assets are $50,000,000 and its current liabilities are $40,000,000, then its _____ would be $50,000,000 divided by $40,000,000, which equals 1.25.

   a. Times interest earned
   b. Return on capital
   c. Net Interest Income
   d. Current ratio

56. _____ measures the rate of return on the ownership interest (shareholders' equity) of the common stock owners. It measures a firm's efficiency at generating profits from every dollar of shareholders' equity (also known as net assets or assets minus liabilities.) It shows how well a company uses investment dollars to generate earnings growth.
   a. Sortino ratio
   b. Like for like
   c. Return on equity
   d. Return on capital employed

Chapter 3. The Financial Position Statement

57. _____, the Electronic Data-Gathering, Analysis, and Retrieval system, performs automated collection, validation, indexing, acceptance, and forwarding of submissions by companies and others who are required by law to file forms with the U.S. Securities and Exchange Commission (the 'SEC'.) The database is freely available to the public via Web or FTP, typically posting in excess of 3,000 filings per day.

Not all SEC filings by public companies are available on _____.

a. AMEX
b. ABC Television Network
c. AIG
d. EDGAR

58. _____ are defined as identifiable non-monetary assets that cannot be seen, touched or physically measured, which are created through time and/or effort and that are identifiable as a separate asset. There are two primary forms of intangibles - legal intangibles (such as trade secrets (e.g., customer lists), copyrights, patents, trademarks, and goodwill) and competitive intangibles (such as knowledge activities (know-how, knowledge), collaboration activities, leverage activities, and structural activities.) Legal intangibles are known under the generic term intellectual property and generate legal property rights defensible in a court of law.

a. ABC Television Network
b. Overhead
c. AIG
d. Intangible assets

59. _____, also known as property, plant, and equipment (PP&E), is a term used in accountancy for assets and property which cannot easily be converted into cash. This can be compared with current assets such as cash or bank accounts, which are described as liquid assets. In most cases, only tangible assets are referred to as fixed.

a. Minority interest
b. Subledger
c. Bankruptcy prediction
d. Fixed asset

Chapter 4. The Income Statement

1. The _____ is a private, not-for-profit organization whose primary purpose is to develop generally accepted accounting principles (GAAP) within the United States in the public's interest. The Securities and Exchange Commission (SEC) designated the _____ as the organization responsible for setting accounting standards for public companies in the U.S. It was created in 1973, replacing the Accounting Principles Board and the Committee on Accounting Procedure of the American Institute of Certified Public Accountants. The _____'s mission is 'to establish and improve standards of financial accounting and reporting for the guidance and education of the public, including issuers, auditors, and users of financial information.'

The _____ is not a governmental body.

   a. Fannie Mae
   b. Governmental Accounting Standards Board
   c. Public company
   d. Financial Accounting Standards Board

2. In economics, _____ or _____ goods or real _____ refers to factors of production used to create goods or services that are not themselves significantly consumed (though they may depreciate) in the production process. _____ goods may be acquired with money or financial _____. In finance and accounting, _____ generally refers to financial wealth, especially that used to start or maintain a business.
   a. Capital
   b. Vyborg Appeal
   c. Screening
   d. Disclosure

3. _____ is that which is owed; usually referencing assets owed, but the term can also cover moral obligations and other interactions not requiring money. In the case of assets, _____ is a means of using future purchasing power in the present before a summation has been earned. Some companies and corporations use _____ as a part of their overall corporate finance strategy.
   a. Debt
   b. Lender
   c. Debenture
   d. Loan

4. _____ is a company's financial statement that indicates how the revenue is transformed into the net income The purpose of the _____ is to show managers and investors whether the company made or lost money during the period being reported.

The important thing to remember about an _____ is that it represents a period of time.

a. AMEX
b. AIG
c. Income statement
d. ABC Television Network

5. _____ is an open standard which supports information modeling and the expression of semantic meaning commonly required in business reporting. _____ is XML-based. It uses the XML syntax and related XML technologies such as XML Schema, XLink, XPath, and Namespaces to articulate this semantic meaning. One use of _____ is to define and exchange financial information, such as a financial statement.

a. 3M Company
b. BMC Software, Inc.
c. BNSF Railway
d. XBRL

6. In economics, business, retail, and accounting, a _____ is the value of money that has been used up to produce something, and hence is not available for use anymore. In economics, a _____ is an alternative that is given up as a result of a decision. In business, the _____ may be one of acquisition, in which case the amount of money expended to acquire it is counted as _____.

a. Cost of quality
b. Cost allocation
c. Prime cost
d. Cost

7. _____ is the term used to refer to the standard framework of guidelines for financial accounting used in any given jurisdiction. _____ includes the standards, conventions, and rules accountants follow in recording and summarizing transactions, and in the preparation of financial statements.

Financial accounting information must be assembled and reported objectively.

a. Generally accepted accounting principles
b. Current asset
c. General ledger
d. Long-term liabilities

8. _____ is a fee paid on borrowed assets. It is the price paid for the use of borrowed money, or, money earned by deposited funds .Assets that are sometimes lent with _____ include money, shares, consumer goods through hire purchase, major assets such as aircraft, and even entire factories in finance lease arrangements. The _____ is calculated upon the value of the assets in the same manner as upon money.

a. Interest
b. AIG
c. Insolvency
d. ABC Television Network

9. The word _____ indicates that a party, or proprietor, exercises private ownership, control or use over an item of property
   a. BMC Software, Inc.
   b. 3M Company
   c. BNSF Railway
   d. Proprietary

10. _____ is concerned with the provisions and use of accounting information to managers within organizations, to provide them with the basis to make informed business decisions that will allow them to be better equipped in their management and control functions.

In contrast to financial accountancy information, _____ information is:

- usually confidential and used by management, instead of publicly reported;
- forward-looking, instead of historical;
- pragmatically computed using extensive management information systems and internal controls, instead of complying with accounting standards.

This is because of the different emphasis: _____ information is used within an organization, typically for decision-making.

   a. Management accounting
   b. Nonassurance services
   c. Grenzplankostenrechnung
   d. Governmental accounting

11. _____ is the planning process used to determine whether a firm's long term investments such as new machinery, replacement machinery, new plants, new products, and research development projects are worth pursuing. It is budget for major capital, or investment, expenditures.

Chapter 4. The Income Statement

Many formal methods are used in _____, including the techniques such as

- Net present value
- Profitability index
- Internal rate of return
- Modified Internal Rate of Return
- Equivalent annuity

These methods use the incremental cash flows from each potential investment, or project. Techniques based on accounting earnings and accounting rules are sometimes used - though economists consider this to be improper - such as the accounting rate of return, and 'return on investment.' Simplified and hybrid methods are used as well, such as payback period and discounted payback period.

a. Capital Budgeting
b. Cash flow
c. Gross profit
d. Preferred stock

12. _____ is the value on a given date of a future payment or series of future payments, discounted to reflect the time value of money and other factors such as investment risk. _____ calculations are widely used in business and economics to provide a means to compare cash flows at different times on a meaningful 'like to like' basis.

The most commonly applied model of the time value of money is compound interest.

a. Future value
b. Net present value
c. 3M Company
d. Present value

13. A _____ is a contract conferring a right on one person to possess property belonging to another person (called a landlord or lessor) to the exclusion of the owner landlord. It is a rental agreement between landlord and tenant. The relationship between the tenant and the landlord is called a tenancy, and the right to possession by the tenant is sometimes called a leasehold interest.
   a. Federal Sentencing Guidelines
   b. Robinson-Patman Act
   c. Model Code of Professional Responsibility
   d. Lease

Chapter 4. The Income Statement

14. The _____ is the former authoritative body of the American Institute of Certified Public Accountants (AICPA.) It was created by the American Institute of Certified Public Accountants in 1959 and issued pronouncements on accounting principles until 1973, when it was replaced by the Financial Accounting Standards Board (FASB.)

The _____ was disbanded in the hopes that the smaller, fully-independent FASB could more effectively create accounting standards.

   a. American Payroll Association
   b. Accounting Principles Board
   c. International Federation of Accountants
   d. Institute of Management Accountants

15. A _____ is a fungible, negotiable instrument representing financial value. they are broadly categorized into debt securities (such as banknotes, bonds and debentures), and equity securities; e.g., common stocks. The company or other entity issuing the _____ is called the issuer.
   a. Tracking stock
   b. Security
   c. 3M Company
   d. BMC Software, Inc.

16. The U.S. _____ is an independent agency of the United States government which holds primary responsibility for enforcing the federal securities laws and regulating the securities industry, the nation's stock and options exchanges, and other electronic securities markets. The SEC was created by section 4 of the Securities Exchange Act of 1934 (now codified as 15 U.S.C. §Â§ 78d and commonly referred to as the 1934 Act.)
   a. 3M Company
   b. BMC Software, Inc.
   c. BNSF Railway
   d. Securities and Exchange Commission

17. _____ is a term used in accounting, economics and finance to spread the cost of an asset over the span of several years.

In simple words we can say that _____ is the reduction in the value of an asset due to usage, passage of time, wear and tear, technological outdating or obsolescence, depletion, inadequacy, rot, rust, decay or other such factors.

In accounting, _____ is a term used to describe any method of attributing the historical or purchase cost of an asset across its useful life, roughly corresponding to normal wear and tear.

Chapter 4. The Income Statement

a. Depreciation
b. General ledger
c. Current asset
d. Net profit

18. _____ is a strategic management responsibility that integrates finance, communication, marketing and securities law compliance to enable the most effective two-way communication between a company, the financial community, and other constituencies, which ultimately contributes to a company's securities achieving fair valuation. The term describes the department of a company devoted to handling inquiries from shareholders and investors, as well as others who might be interested in a company's stock or financial stability.

a. ABC Television Network
b. AIG
c. AMEX
d. Investor Relations

19. _____ is equal to the income that a firm has after subtracting costs and expenses from the total revenue. _____ can be distributed among holders of common stock as a dividend or held by the firm as retained earnings.

The items deducted will typically include tax expense, financing expense (interest expense), and minority interest. Likewise, preferred stock dividends will be subtracted too, though they are not an expense.

a. Generally accepted accounting principles
b. Long-term liabilities
c. Matching principle
d. Net income

20. In economics, a _____ is a mechanism that allows people to easily buy and sell (trade) financial securities (such as stocks and bonds), commodities (such as precious metals or agricultural goods), and other fungible items of value at low transaction costs and at prices that reflect the efficient-market hypothesis.

They have evolved significantly over several hundred years and are undergoing constant innovation to improve liquidity.

Both general markets (where many commodities are traded) and specialized markets (where only one commodity is traded) exist.

Chapter 4. The Income Statement

a. Transfer agent
b. Financial Market
c. Mark-to-market
d. Spot rate

21. A _____ is any one of a variety of different systems, institutions, procedures, social relations and infrastructures whereby persons trade, and goods and services are exchanged, forming part of the economy. It is an arrangement that allows buyers and sellers to exchange things. _____s vary in size, range, geographic scale, location, types and variety of human communities, as well as the types of goods and services traded.

a. Market Failure
b. Market
c. Perfect competition
d. Recession

22. An _____ is a tax levied on the financial income of people, corporations, or other legal entities. Various _____ systems exist, with varying degrees of tax incidence. Income taxation can be progressive, proportional, or regressive.

a. Implied level of government service
b. Ordinary income
c. Income tax
d. Individual Retirement Arrangement

23. In finance, a _____ is a debt security, in which the authorized issuer owes the holders a debt and, depending on the terms of the _____, is obliged to pay interest (the coupon) and/or to repay the principal at a later date, termed maturity. It is a formal contract to repay borrowed money with interest at fixed intervals.

Thus a _____ is like a loan: the issuer is the borrower, the _____ holder is the lender, and the coupon is the interest.

a. Revenue bonds
b. Zero-coupon bond
c. Coupon rate
d. Bond

24. In finance, a _____ is a type of bond that can be converted into shares of stock in the issuing company, usually at some pre-announced ratio. It is a hybrid security with debt- and equity-like features. Although it typically has a low coupon rate, the holder is compensated with the ability to convert the bond to common stock, usually at a substantial discount to the stock's market value.

a. Zero-coupon bond
b. Convertible bond
c. Zero-coupon
d. Coupon rate

25. An _____ is the price a borrower pays for the use of money they do not own, for instance a small company might borrow from a bank to kick start their business, and the return a lender receives for deferring the use of funds, by lending it to the borrower. _____s are normally expressed as a percentage rate over the period of one year.

_____s targets are also a vital tool of monetary policy and are used to control variables like investment, inflation, and unemployment.

a. AIG
b. AMEX
c. ABC Television Network
d. Interest rate

26. Project _____: The project _____ is a prediction of the costs associated with a particular company project. These costs include labor, materials, and other related expenses. The project _____ is often broken down into specific tasks, with task _____s assigned to each.
a. Budget
b. BMC Software, Inc.
c. BNSF Railway
d. 3M Company

27. The _____ is a Cabinet-level office, and is the largest office within the Executive Office of the President of the United States (EOP.) It is an important conduit by which the White House oversees the activities of federal agencies. OMB is tasked with giving expert advice to senior White House officials on a range of topics relating to federal policy, management, legislative, regulatory, and budgetary issues.
a. Alaska Air Group
b. Office of Management and Budget
c. Analysis of variance
d. AT'T Wireless Services, Inc.

28. In management accounting, _____ establishes budget and actual cost of operations, processes, departments or product and the analysis of variances, profitability or social use of funds. Managers use _____ to support decision-making to cut a company's costs and improve profitability. As a form of management accounting, _____ need not follow standards such as GAAP, because its primary use is for internal managers, rather than outside users, and what to compute is instead decided pragmatically.

a. Marginal cost
b. Cost-volume-profit analysis
c. Prime cost
d. Cost accounting

29. The _____ is a performance management tool which began as a concept for measuring whether the smaller-scale operational activities of a company are aligned with its larger-scale objectives in terms of vision and strategy.

By focusing not only on financial outcomes but also on the operational, marketing and developmental inputs to these, the _____ helps provide a more comprehensive view of a business, which in turn helps organizations act in their best long-term interests. This tool is also being used to address business response to climate change and greenhouse gas emissions.

a. Best practice
b. Trustee
c. Balanced scorecard
d. Management by objectives

30. The _____ founded on April 1, 2001 is the successor of the International Accounting Standards Committee (IASC) founded in June 1973 in London. It is responsible for developing the International Financial Reporting Standards (new name for the International Accounting Standards issued after 2001), and promoting the use and application of these standards.

The _____ is an independent, privately-funded accounting standard-setter based in London, UK.

a. Institute of Management Accountants
b. Emerging technologies
c. Information Systems Audit and Control Association
d. International Accounting Standards Board

31. In accounting, _____ has a very specific meaning. It is an outflow of cash or other valuable assets from a person or company to another person or company. This outflow of cash is generally one side of a trade for products or services that have equal or better current or future value to the buyer than to the seller.

a. ABC Television Network
b. AIG
c. Expense
d. AMEX

32. _____ is a financial metric which represents operating liquidity available to a business. Along with fixed assets such as plant and equipment, _____ is considered a part of operating capital. It is calculated as current assets minus current liabilities.
   a. Working capital management
   b. Working capital
   c. BMC Software, Inc.
   d. 3M Company

33. The term _____ or superannuation refers to a pension granted upon retirement. They may be set up by employers, insurance companies, the government or other institutions such as employer associations or trade unions.
   a. Wage
   b. BMC Software, Inc.
   c. 3M Company
   d. Retirement plan

34. _____ is an umbrella term which refers to the various accounting systems used by various public sector entities. In the United States, for instance, there are two levels of government which follow different accounting standards set forth by independent, private sector boards. At the federal level, the Federal Accounting Standards Advisory Board (FASAB) sets forth the accounting standards to follow.
   a. Management accounting
   b. Product control
   c. Nonassurance services
   d. Governmental Accounting

35. The _____ is currently the source of generally accepted accounting principles (GAAP) used by State and Local governments in the [[United States of America]]. As with most of the entities involved in creating GAAP in the United States, it is a private, non-governmental organization.

The _____ is subject to oversight by the Financial Accounting Foundation (FAF), which selects the members of the _____ and the Financial Accounting Standards Board, and funds both organizations.

a. National Conference of Commissioners on Uniform State Laws
b. Multinational corporation
c. Fannie Mae
d. Governmental Accounting Standards Board

Chapter 5. Statement of Changes in Equity

1. The _____ is a private, not-for-profit organization whose primary purpose is to develop generally accepted accounting principles (GAAP) within the United States in the public's interest. The Securities and Exchange Commission (SEC) designated the _____ as the organization responsible for setting accounting standards for public companies in the U.S. It was created in 1973, replacing the Accounting Principles Board and the Committee on Accounting Procedure of the American Institute of Certified Public Accountants. The _____'s mission is 'to establish and improve standards of financial accounting and reporting for the guidance and education of the public, including issuers, auditors, and users of financial information.'

    The _____ is not a governmental body.

    a. Governmental Accounting Standards Board
    b. Financial Accounting Standards Board
    c. Fannie Mae
    d. Public company

2. The _____ is currently the source of generally accepted accounting principles (GAAP) used by State and Local governments in the [[United States of America]]. As with most of the entities involved in creating GAAP in the United States, it is a private, non-governmental organization.

    The _____ is subject to oversight by the Financial Accounting Foundation (FAF), which selects the members of the _____ and the Financial Accounting Standards Board, and funds both organizations.

    a. National Conference of Commissioners on Uniform State Laws
    b. Multinational corporation
    c. Fannie Mae
    d. Governmental Accounting Standards Board

3. _____ is a strategic management responsibility that integrates finance, communication, marketing and securities law compliance to enable the most effective two-way communication between a company, the financial community, and other constituencies, which ultimately contributes to a company's securities achieving fair valuation. The term describes the department of a company devoted to handling inquiries from shareholders and investors, as well as others who might be interested in a company's stock or financial stability.
    a. AMEX
    b. ABC Television Network
    c. AIG
    d. Investor Relations

4. _____ are formal records of a business' financial activities.

    In British English, including United Kingdom company law, _____ are often referred to as accounts, although the term _____ is also used, particularly by accountants.

Chapter 5. Statement of Changes in Equity

_____ provide an overview of a business' financial condition in both short and long term.

a. Statement of retained earnings
b. Notes to the financial statements
c. Financial statements
d. 3M Company

5. _____ is equal to the income that a firm has after subtracting costs and expenses from the total revenue. _____ can be distributed among holders of common stock as a dividend or held by the firm as retained earnings.

The items deducted will typically include tax expense, financing expense (interest expense), and minority interest. Likewise, preferred stock dividends will be subtracted too, though they are not an expense.

a. Generally accepted accounting principles
b. Long-term liabilities
c. Matching principle
d. Net income

6. Project _____: The project _____ is a prediction of the costs associated with a particular company project. These costs include labor, materials, and other related expenses. The project _____ is often broken down into specific tasks, with task _____s assigned to each.

a. BNSF Railway
b. Budget
c. 3M Company
d. BMC Software, Inc.

7. The _____ is a Cabinet-level office, and is the largest office within the Executive Office of the President of the United States (EOP.) It is an important conduit by which the White House oversees the activities of federal agencies. OMB is tasked with giving expert advice to senior White House officials on a range of topics relating to federal policy, management, legislative, regulatory, and budgetary issues.

a. Analysis of variance
b. Alaska Air Group
c. Office of Management and Budget
d. AT'T Wireless Services, Inc.

Chapter 5. Statement of Changes in Equity

8. In finance, an _____ is a contract between a buyer and a seller that gives the buyer the right--but not the obligation--to buy or to sell a particular asset (the underlying asset) at a later time at an agreed price. In return for granting the _____, the seller collects a payment (the premium) from the buyer. A call _____ gives the buyer the right to buy the underlying asset; a put _____ gives the buyer of the _____ the right to sell the underlying asset.
   a. AMEX
   b. AIG
   c. ABC Television Network
   d. Option

9. _____ is a specific term used in companies' financial reporting from the company-whole point of view. Because that use excludes the effects of changing ownership interest, an economic measure of _____ is necessary for financial analysis from the shareholders' point of view

   _____ is defined by the Financial Accounting Standards Board, or FASB, as 'the change in equity [net assets] of a business enterprise during a period from transactions and other events and circumstances from nonowner sources. It includes all changes in equity during a period except those resulting from investments by owners and distributions to owners.'

   _____ is the sum of net income and other items that must bypass the income statement because they have not been realized, including items like an unrealized holding gain or loss from available for sale securities and foreign currency translation gains or losses.

   a. BNSF Railway
   b. 3M Company
   c. Comprehensive income
   d. BMC Software, Inc.

10. _____ are the earnings returned on the initial investment amount.

In the US, the Financial Accounting Standards Board (FASB) requires companies' income statements to report _____ for each of the major categories of the income statement: continuing operations, discontinued operations, extraordinary items, and net income.

The _____ formula does not include preferred dividends for categories outside of continued operations and net income.

Chapter 5. Statement of Changes in Equity

a. Average accounting return
b. Invested capital
c. Earnings yield
d. Earnings per share

11. _____ is the term used to refer to the standard framework of guidelines for financial accounting used in any given jurisdiction. _____ includes the standards, conventions, and rules accountants follow in recording and summarizing transactions, and in the preparation of financial statements.

Financial accounting information must be assembled and reported objectively.

a. Long-term liabilities
b. Current asset
c. General ledger
d. Generally accepted accounting principles

12. The _____ was a predecessor of the Accounting Principles Board, itself a predecessor to the Financial Accounting Standards Board in the United States. Its formation and activities were early efforts to rationalize and legitimize the reporting of business performance. However, it is widely regarded as having failed.

a. Consolidated financial statements
b. Price variance
c. Lump sum
d. Committee on Accounting Procedure

13. _____, the Electronic Data-Gathering, Analysis, and Retrieval system, performs automated collection, validation, indexing, acceptance, and forwarding of submissions by companies and others who are required by law to file forms with the U.S. Securities and Exchange Commission (the 'SEC'.) The database is freely available to the public via Web or FTP, typically posting in excess of 3,000 filings per day.

Not all SEC filings by public companies are available on _____.

a. ABC Television Network
b. EDGAR
c. AIG
d. AMEX

14. _____ is the balance of the amounts of cash being received and paid by a business during a defined period of time, sometimes tied to a specific project. Measurement of _____ can be used

- to evaluate the state or performance of a business or project.
- to determine problems with liquidity. Being profitable does not necessarily mean being liquid. A company can fail because of a shortage of cash, even while profitable.
- to project rate of returns. The time of _____s into and out of projects are used as inputs to financial models such as internal rate of return, and net present value.
- to examine income or growth of a business when it is believed that accrual accounting concepts do not represent economic realities. Alternately, _____ can be used to 'validate' the net income generated by accrual accounting.

_____ as a generic term may be used differently depending on context, and certain _____ definitions may be adapted by analysts and users for their own uses. Common terms include operating _____ and free _____.

a. Controlling interest
b. Commercial paper
c. Cash flow
d. Flow-through entity

15. The term '_____' refers to the concept of collecting information and attempting to spot a pattern in the information. In some fields of study, the term '_____' has more formally-defined meanings.

In project management _____ is a mathematical technique that uses historical results to predict future outcome.

a. Multicollinearity
b. Trend analysis
c. 3M Company
d. Regression analysis

16. The _____ is a 'voluntary organization of persons interested in accounting education and research'. It was formed in 1916. Its main publication, the The Accounting Review, was first published in 1926.
a. Australian Accounting Standards Board
b. Institute of Management Accountants
c. International Accounting Standards Board
d. American Accounting Association

Chapter 6. The Cash Flow Statement

1. The _____ is a private, not-for-profit organization whose primary purpose is to develop generally accepted accounting principles (GAAP) within the United States in the public's interest. The Securities and Exchange Commission (SEC) designated the _____ as the organization responsible for setting accounting standards for public companies in the U.S. It was created in 1973, replacing the Accounting Principles Board and the Committee on Accounting Procedure of the American Institute of Certified Public Accountants. The _____'s mission is 'to establish and improve standards of financial accounting and reporting for the guidance and education of the public, including issuers, auditors, and users of financial information.'

The _____ is not a governmental body.

   a. Fannie Mae
   b. Financial Accounting Standards Board
   c. Public company
   d. Governmental Accounting Standards Board

2. _____ is the balance of the amounts of cash being received and paid by a business during a defined period of time, sometimes tied to a specific project. Measurement of _____ can be used

   - to evaluate the state or performance of a business or project.
   - to determine problems with liquidity. Being profitable does not necessarily mean being liquid. A company can fail because of a shortage of cash, even while profitable.
   - to project rate of returns. The time of _____s into and out of projects are used as inputs to financial models such as internal rate of return, and net present value.
   - to examine income or growth of a business when it is believed that accrual accounting concepts do not represent economic realities. Alternately, _____ can be used to 'validate' the net income generated by accrual accounting.

   _____ as a generic term may be used differently depending on context, and certain _____ definitions may be adapted by analysts and users for their own uses. Common terms include operating _____ and free _____.

   a. Controlling interest
   b. Commercial paper
   c. Flow-through entity
   d. Cash flow

3. In financial accounting, a _____ or Statement of cash flows is a financial statement that shows a company's flow of cash. The money coming into the business is called cash inflow, and money going out from the business is called cash outflow. The statement shows how changes in balance sheet and income accounts affect cash and cash equivalents, and breaks the analysis down to operating, investing, and financing activities.

a. Cash flow statement
b. 3M Company
c. BNSF Railway
d. BMC Software, Inc.

4. A _____ has several related meanings:

   - a daily record of events or business; a private _____ is usually referred to as a diary.
   - a newspaper or other periodical, in the literal sense of one published each day;
   - many publications issued at stated intervals, such as magazines, or scholarly academic _____s, or the record of the transactions of a society, are often called _____s. Although _____ is sometimes used, erroneously, as a synonym for 'magazine,' in academic use, a _____ refers to a serious, scholarly publication, most often peer-reviewed. A non-scholarly magazine written for an educated audience about an industry or an area of professional activity is usually called a professional magazine.

The word 'journalist' for one whose business is writing for the public press has been in use since the end of the 17th century.

Open access _____s are scholarly _____s that are available to the reader without financial or other barrier other than access to the internet itself. Some are subsidized, and some require payment on behalf of the author. Subsidized _____s are financed by an academic institution or a government information center.

a. Journal
b. BNSF Railway
c. 3M Company
d. BMC Software, Inc.

5. In business and accounting, _____ are everything of value that is owned by a person or company. It is a claim on the property your income of a borrower. The balance sheet of a firm records the monetary value of the _____ owned by the firm.
   a. Assets
   b. Earnings before interest, taxes, depreciation and amortization
   c. Accounts receivable
   d. Accrual basis accounting

6. _____ is a legally declared inability or impairment of ability of an individual or organization to pay its creditors. Creditors may file a _____ petition against a debtor ('involuntary _____') in an effort to recoup a portion of what they are owed or initiate a restructuring. In the majority of cases, however, _____ is initiated by the debtor (a 'voluntary _____' that is filed by the bankrupt individual or organization.)

Chapter 6. The Cash Flow Statement

a. Bankruptcy protection
b. 3M Company
c. BMC Software, Inc.
d. Bankruptcy

7. In financial accounting, a _____ is defined as an obligation of an entity arising from past transactions or events, the settlement of which may result in the transfer or use of assets, provision of services or other yielding of economic benefits in the future.

a. Vested
b. Corporate governance
c. Liability
d. False Claims Act

8. _____ is a specific term used in companies' financial reporting from the company-whole point of view. Because that use excludes the effects of changing ownership interest, an economic measure of _____ is necessary for financial analysis from the shareholders' point of view

_____ is defined by the Financial Accounting Standards Board, or FASB, as 'the change in equity [net assets] of a business enterprise during a period from transactions and other events and circumstances from nonowner sources. It includes all changes in equity during a period except those resulting from investments by owners and distributions to owners.'

_____ is the sum of net income and other items that must bypass the income statement because they have not been realized, including items like an unrealized holding gain or loss from available for sale securities and foreign currency translation gains or losses.

a. 3M Company
b. Comprehensive income
c. BNSF Railway
d. BMC Software, Inc.

9. An _____ is a practitioner of accountancy, which is the measurement, disclosure or provision of assurance about financial information that helps managers, investors, tax authorities and other decision makers make resource allocation decisions.

The word '_____' is derived from the French 'Compter' which took its origin from the Latin 'Computare'. The word was formerly written in English as 'Accomptant', but in process of time the word, which was always pronounced by dropping the 'p', became gradually changed both in pronunciation and in orthography to its present form.

Chapter 6. The Cash Flow Statement

a. AIG
b. AMEX
c. ABC Television Network
d. Accountant

10. The _____ is the national, professional association of CPAs in the United States, with more than 330,000 members, including CPAs in business and industry, public practice, government, and education; student affiliates; and international associates. It sets ethical standards for the profession and U.S. auditing standards for audits of private companies; federal, state and local governments; and non-profit organizations.

Approximately 40% of its members are engaged in the practice of public accounting, in areas such as auditing, accounting, taxation, general business consulting, business valuation, personal financial planning and business technology.

a. Other postemployment benefits
b. ABC Television Network
c. AIG
d. American Institute of Certified Public Accountants

11. _____ is the statutory title of qualified accountants in the United States who have passed the Uniform _____ Examination and have met additional state education and experience requirements for certification as a _____. Individuals who have passed the Exam but have not either accomplished the required on-the-job experience or have previously met it but in the meantime have lapsed their continuing professional education are, in many states, permitted the designation '_____ Inactive' or an equivalent phrase. In most U.S. states, only _____s who are licensed are able to provide to the public attestation (including auditing) opinions on financial statements.

a. Certified General Accountant
b. Chartered Certified Accountant
c. Chartered Accountant
d. Certified Public Accountant

12. The term '_____' refers to the concept of collecting information and attempting to spot a pattern in the information. In some fields of study, the term '_____' has more formally-defined meanings.

In project management _____ is a mathematical technique that uses historical results to predict future outcome.

Chapter 6. The Cash Flow Statement

a. Multicollinearity
b. 3M Company
c. Regression analysis
d. Trend analysis

13. _____ is an open standard which supports information modeling and the expression of semantic meaning commonly required in business reporting. _____ is XML-based. It uses the XML syntax and related XML technologies such as XML Schema, XLink, XPath, and Namespaces to articulate this semantic meaning. One use of _____ is to define and exchange financial information, such as a financial statement.

 a. XBRL
 b. BMC Software, Inc.
 c. 3M Company
 d. BNSF Railway

14. In financial accounting, _____ , cash flow provided by operations or cash flow from operating activities, refers to the amount of cash a company generates from the revenues it brings in, excluding costs associated with long-term investment on capital items or investment in securities.

_____ = Cash generated from operations less taxation and interest paid, investment income received and less dividends paid gives rise to _____s per International Financial Reporting Standards.

To calculate cash generated from operations, one must calculate cash generated from customers and cash paid to suppliers.

 a. AIG
 b. AMEX
 c. ABC Television Network
 d. Operating cash flow

15. _____ was founded in June 1973 in London and replaced by the International Accounting Standards Board on April 1, 2001. It was responsible for developing the International Accounting Standards and promoting the use and application of these standards.

Chapter 6. The Cash Flow Statement 67

The _____ was founded as a result of an agreement between accountancy bodies in the following countries:

- Australia (Institute of Chartered Accountants in Australia (ICAA) and the CPA Australia (formerly known as Australian Society of Certified Practising Accountants (ASCPA))
- Canada (Canadian Institute of Chartered Accountants (CICA))
- France (Ordre des Experts Comptable et des Comptables Agrees (Order of Accounting Experts and Qualified Accountants))
- Germany and the Wirtschaftsprüferkammer (WPK) (Chamber of Auditors))
- Japan Nihon Kouninkaikeishi Kyoukai)
- Mexico (Instituto Mexicano de Contadores Publicos (IMCP) (Mexican Institute of Public Accountants)) (removed from the board in 1987 due to non-payment of dues; resumed in 1995.)
- the Netherlands (Nederlands Instituut van Registeraccountants (NIVRA)

(Netherlands Institute of Registered Auditors))

- the United Kingdom and Ireland (counted as one) (Institute of Chartered Accountants in England and Wales (ICAEW), Institute of Chartered Accountants of Scotland (ICAS), Institute of Chartered Accountants in Ireland (ICAI), Association of Certified Accountants, Institute of Cost and Management Accountants, and the Institute of Municipal Treasurers and Accountants)
- the United States of America (American Institute of Certified Public Accountants (AICPA))

The Institute of Chartered Accountants of Nigeria became an associate member in 1976 and a member of the board from 1978 to 1987.

The National Council of Chartered Accountants (South Africa) became an associate member in 1974 and joined the board in 1978.

   a. International Accounting Standards Board
   b. International Accounting Standards Committee
   c. American Accounting Association
   d. American Payroll Association

Chapter 7. Nonprofit Accounting

1. The _____ is a private, not-for-profit organization whose primary purpose is to develop generally accepted accounting principles (GAAP) within the United States in the public's interest. The Securities and Exchange Commission (SEC) designated the _____ as the organization responsible for setting accounting standards for public companies in the U.S. It was created in 1973, replacing the Accounting Principles Board and the Committee on Accounting Procedure of the American Institute of Certified Public Accountants. The _____'s mission is 'to establish and improve standards of financial accounting and reporting for the guidance and education of the public, including issuers, auditors, and users of financial information.'

The _____ is not a governmental body.

   a. Public company
   b. Financial Accounting Standards Board
   c. Fannie Mae
   d. Governmental Accounting Standards Board

2. An _____ is a practitioner of accountancy, which is the measurement, disclosure or provision of assurance about financial information that helps managers, investors, tax authorities and other decision makers make resource allocation decisions.

The word '_____' is derived from the French 'Compter' which took its origin from the Latin 'Computare'. The word was formerly written in English as 'Accomptant', but in process of time the word, which was always pronounced by dropping the 'p', became gradually changed both in pronunciation and in orthography to its present form.

   a. ABC Television Network
   b. AIG
   c. AMEX
   d. Accountant

3. The _____ is the national, professional association of CPAs in the United States, with more than 330,000 members, including CPAs in business and industry, public practice, government, and education; student affiliates; and international associates. It sets ethical standards for the profession and U.S. auditing standards for audits of private companies; federal, state and local governments; and non-profit organizations.

Approximately 40% of its members are engaged in the practice of public accounting, in areas such as auditing, accounting, taxation, general business consulting, business valuation, personal financial planning and business technology.

Chapter 7. Nonprofit Accounting

a. AIG
b. ABC Television Network
c. Other postemployment benefits
d. American Institute of Certified Public Accountants

4. _____ is the statutory title of qualified accountants in the United States who have passed the Uniform _____ Examination and have met additional state education and experience requirements for certification as a _____. Individuals who have passed the Exam but have not either accomplished the required on-the-job experience or have previously met it but in the meantime have lapsed their continuing professional education are, in many states, permitted the designation '_____ Inactive' or an equivalent phrase. In most U.S. states, only _____s who are licensed are able to provide to the public attestation (including auditing) opinions on financial statements.

a. Certified General Accountant
b. Certified Public Accountant
c. Chartered Accountant
d. Chartered Certified Accountant

5. The general definition of an _____ is an evaluation of a person, organization, system, process, project or product. _____s are performed to ascertain the validity and reliability of information; also to provide an assessment of a system's internal control. The goal of an _____ is to express an opinion on the person/organization/system (etc) in question, under evaluation based on work done on a test basis.

a. Institute of Chartered Accountants of India
b. Audit regime
c. Audit
d. Assurance service

6. _____, the Electronic Data-Gathering, Analysis, and Retrieval system, performs automated collection, validation, indexing, acceptance, and forwarding of submissions by companies and others who are required by law to file forms with the U.S. Securities and Exchange Commission (the 'SEC'.) The database is freely available to the public via Web or FTP, typically posting in excess of 3,000 filings per day.

Not all SEC filings by public companies are available on _____.

a. AIG
b. AMEX
c. ABC Television Network
d. EDGAR

Chapter 7. Nonprofit Accounting

7. In economics, a _____ is a mechanism that allows people to easily buy and sell (trade) financial securities (such as stocks and bonds), commodities (such as precious metals or agricultural goods), and other fungible items of value at low transaction costs and at prices that reflect the efficient-market hypothesis.

They have evolved significantly over several hundred years and are undergoing constant innovation to improve liquidity.

Both general markets (where many commodities are traded) and specialized markets (where only one commodity is traded) exist.

a. Mark-to-market
b. Transfer agent
c. Spot rate
d. Financial Market

8. A _____ is any one of a variety of different systems, institutions, procedures, social relations and infrastructures whereby persons trade, and goods and services are exchanged, forming part of the economy. It is an arrangement that allows buyers and sellers to exchange things. _____s vary in size, range, geographic scale, location, types and variety of human communities, as well as the types of goods and services traded.

a. Market Failure
b. Perfect competition
c. Recession
d. Market

9. In finance, a _____ is a debt security, in which the authorized issuer owes the holders a debt and, depending on the terms of the _____, is obliged to pay interest (the coupon) and/or to repay the principal at a later date, termed maturity. It is a formal contract to repay borrowed money with interest at fixed intervals.

Thus a _____ is like a loan: the issuer is the borrower, the _____ holder is the lender, and the coupon is the interest.

a. Bond
b. Revenue bonds
c. Coupon rate
d. Zero-coupon bond

10. Net income is informally called the _____ because it is typically found on the last line of a company's income statement. A related term is top line, meaning revenue, which forms the first line of the account statement.

An equation for net income in merchandising:

Net income or net loss =Revenue - Cost of goods sold - Sales discounts - Sales returns and allowances - Expenses - Minority interest - Preferred stock dividends

a. Payroll
b. Current asset
c. Pro forma
d. Bottom line

11. _____ is a specific term used in companies' financial reporting from the company-whole point of view. Because that use excludes the effects of changing ownership interest, an economic measure of _____ is necessary for financial analysis from the shareholders' point of view

_____ is defined by the Financial Accounting Standards Board, or FASB, as 'the change in equity [net assets] of a business enterprise during a period from transactions and other events and circumstances from nonowner sources. It includes all changes in equity during a period except those resulting from investments by owners and distributions to owners.'

_____ is the sum of net income and other items that must bypass the income statement because they have not been realized, including items like an unrealized holding gain or loss from available for sale securities and foreign currency translation gains or losses.

a. 3M Company
b. Comprehensive income
c. BNSF Railway
d. BMC Software, Inc.

12. _____ is the term used to refer to the standard framework of guidelines for financial accounting used in any given jurisdiction. _____ includes the standards, conventions, and rules accountants follow in recording and summarizing transactions, and in the preparation of financial statements.

Financial accounting information must be assembled and reported objectively.

a. General ledger
b. Generally accepted accounting principles
c. Current asset
d. Long-term liabilities

13. A _____ is the transfer of wealth from one party (such as a person or company) to another. A _____ is usually made in exchange for the provision of goods, services or both, or to fulfill a legal obligation.

The simplest and oldest form of _____ is barter, the exchange of one good or service for another.

a. Payment
b. BMC Software, Inc.
c. 3M Company
d. Payee

14. _____ is an open standard which supports information modeling and the expression of semantic meaning commonly required in business reporting. _____ is XML-based. It uses the XML syntax and related XML technologies such as XML Schema, XLink, XPath, and Namespaces to articulate this semantic meaning. One use of _____ is to define and exchange financial information, such as a financial statement.

a. 3M Company
b. XBRL
c. BNSF Railway
d. BMC Software, Inc.

15. In business and accounting, _____ are everything of value that is owned by a person or company. It is a claim on the property your income of a borrower. The balance sheet of a firm records the monetary value of the _____ owned by the firm.

a. Assets
b. Accounts receivable
c. Accrual basis accounting
d. Earnings before interest, taxes, depreciation and amortization

16. _____, also called fair price (in a commonplace conflation of the two distinct concepts), is a concept used in finance and economics, defined as a rational and unbiased estimate of the potential market price of a good, service, or asset, taking into account such objective factors as:

- acquisition/production/distribution costs, replacement costs, or costs of close substitutes
- actual utility at a given level of development of social productive capability
- supply vs. demand

Chapter 7. Nonprofit Accounting

and subjective factors such as

- risk characteristics
- cost of capital
- individually perceived utility

In accounting, _____ is used as an estimate of the market value of an asset (or liability) for which a market price cannot be determined (usually because there is no established market for the asset.) Under GAAP (FAS 157), _____ is the amount at which the asset could be bought or sold in a current transaction between willing parties, or transferred to an equivalent party, other than in a liquidation sale. This is used for assets whose carrying value is based on mark-to-market valuations; for assets carried at historical cost, the _____ of the asset is not used. One example of where _____ is an issue is a College kitchen with a cost of $2 million which was built 5 years ago.

a. 3M Company
b. BMC Software, Inc.
c. Fair value
d. BNSF Railway

Chapter 8. State and Local Government Accounting

1. _____ is an umbrella term which refers to the various accounting systems used by various public sector entities. In the United States, for instance, there are two levels of government which follow different accounting standards set forth by independent, private sector boards. At the federal level, the Federal Accounting Standards Advisory Board (FASAB) sets forth the accounting standards to follow.
   a. Product control
   b. Management accounting
   c. Governmental Accounting
   d. Nonassurance services

2. The _____ is currently the source of generally accepted accounting principles (GAAP) used by State and Local governments in the [[United States of America]]. As with most of the entities involved in creating GAAP in the United States, it is a private, non-governmental organization.

   The _____ is subject to oversight by the Financial Accounting Foundation (FAF), which selects the members of the _____ and the Financial Accounting Standards Board, and funds both organizations.

   a. National Conference of Commissioners on Uniform State Laws
   b. Fannie Mae
   c. Governmental Accounting Standards Board
   d. Multinational corporation

3. The _____ is located in Norwalk, Connecticut. It is an independent, organization in the private sector that is responsible for oversight of the Financial Accounting Standards Board (FASB), the Governmental Accounting Standards Board (GASB), and their respective advisory councils.
   a. Financial Accounting Foundation
   b. 3M Company
   c. BNSF Railway
   d. BMC Software, Inc.

4. The _____ is a private, not-for-profit organization whose primary purpose is to develop generally accepted accounting principles (GAAP) within the United States in the public's interest. The Securities and Exchange Commission (SEC) designated the _____ as the organization responsible for setting accounting standards for public companies in the U.S. It was created in 1973, replacing the Accounting Principles Board and the Committee on Accounting Procedure of the American Institute of Certified Public Accountants. The _____'s mission is 'to establish and improve standards of financial accounting and reporting for the guidance and education of the public, including issuers, auditors, and users of financial information.'

   The _____ is not a governmental body.

Chapter 8. State and Local Government Accounting

75

   a. Governmental Accounting Standards Board
   b. Public company
   c. Fannie Mae
   d. Financial Accounting Standards Board

5. In business and accounting, _____ are everything of value that is owned by a person or company. It is a claim on the property your income of a borrower. The balance sheet of a firm records the monetary value of the _____ owned by the firm.
   a. Accrual basis accounting
   b. Assets
   c. Accounts receivable
   d. Earnings before interest, taxes, depreciation and amortization

6. In financial accounting, a _____ is defined as an obligation of an entity arising from past transactions or events, the settlement of which may result in the transfer or use of assets, provision of services or other yielding of economic benefits in the future.
   a. Liability
   b. False Claims Act
   c. Vested
   d. Corporate governance

7. The term '_____' refers to the concept of collecting information and attempting to spot a pattern in the information. In some fields of study, the term '_____' has more formally-defined meanings.

In project management _____ is a mathematical technique that uses historical results to predict future outcome.

   a. 3M Company
   b. Regression analysis
   c. Multicollinearity
   d. Trend analysis

8. _____ of something is, in finance, the adding together of interest or different investments over a period of time such as atoms (1 - the act or process of accruing; 2 - the amount that accrues.) It holds specific meanings in accounting and payroll.

Chapter 8. State and Local Government Accounting

_____, in accounting, describes the accounting method known as _____ basis, whereby revenues and expenses are recognized when they are accrued, i.e. accumulated (earned or incurred), regardless when the actual cash is received or paid out.

a. Assets
b. Accrual
c. Earnings before interest, taxes, depreciation and amortization
d. Accounts receivable

9. _____ is a method of accounting whereby economic activities (rather than cash flow) of financial events are considered, because of two complementary principles, which (together) determine the point, at which expenses and revenues are recognized. According to revenue recognition principle, revenues are realized when earned, whether or not they are received in cash.
a. Accrual
b. Accrued revenue
c. Earnings before interest, taxes, depreciation and amortization
d. Accrual basis accounting

10. _____ are formal records of a business' financial activities.

In British English, including United Kingdom company law, _____ are often referred to as accounts, although the term _____ is also used, particularly by accountants.

_____ provide an overview of a business' financial condition in both short and long term.

a. 3M Company
b. Statement of retained earnings
c. Notes to the financial statements
d. Financial statements

11. The _____ was a predecessor of the Accounting Principles Board, itself a predecessor to the Financial Accounting Standards Board in the United States. Its formation and activities were early efforts to rationalize and legitimize the reporting of business performance. However, it is widely regarded as having failed.
a. Committee on Accounting Procedure
b. Price variance
c. Lump sum
d. Consolidated financial statements

Chapter 8. State and Local Government Accounting

12. In economics, a _____ is a mechanism that allows people to easily buy and sell (trade) financial securities (such as stocks and bonds), commodities (such as precious metals or agricultural goods), and other fungible items of value at low transaction costs and at prices that reflect the efficient-market hypothesis.

They have evolved significantly over several hundred years and are undergoing constant innovation to improve liquidity.

Both general markets (where many commodities are traded) and specialized markets (where only one commodity is traded) exist.

a. Transfer agent
b. Mark-to-market
c. Spot rate
d. Financial Market

13. A _____ is any one of a variety of different systems, institutions, procedures, social relations and infrastructures whereby persons trade, and goods and services are exchanged, forming part of the economy. It is an arrangement that allows buyers and sellers to exchange things. _____s vary in size, range, geographic scale, location, types and variety of human communities, as well as the types of goods and services traded.

a. Market
b. Recession
c. Market Failure
d. Perfect competition

14. In economics, business, retail, and accounting, a _____ is the value of money that has been used up to produce something, and hence is not available for use anymore. In economics, a _____ is an alternative that is given up as a result of a decision. In business, the _____ may be one of acquisition, in which case the amount of money expended to acquire it is counted as _____.

a. Cost of quality
b. Prime cost
c. Cost allocation
d. Cost

15. The general definition of an _____ is an evaluation of a person, organization, system, process, project or product. _____s are performed to ascertain the validity and reliability of information; also to provide an assessment of a system's internal control. The goal of an _____ is to express an opinion on the person/organization/system (etc) in question, under evaluation based on work done on a test basis.

a. Assurance service
b. Institute of Chartered Accountants of India
c. Audit regime
d. Audit

16. In economics, _____ or _____ goods or real _____ refers to factors of production used to create goods or services that are not themselves significantly consumed (though they may depreciate) in the production process. _____ goods may be acquired with money or financial _____. In finance and accounting, _____ generally refers to financial wealth, especially that used to start or maintain a business.
    a. Screening
    b. Vyborg Appeal
    c. Disclosure
    d. Capital

17. _____ is the planning process used to determine whether a firm's long term investments such as new machinery, replacement machinery, new plants, new products, and research development projects are worth pursuing. It is budget for major capital, or investment, expenditures.

Many formal methods are used in _____, including the techniques such as

- Net present value
- Profitability index
- Internal rate of return
- Modified Internal Rate of Return
- Equivalent annuity

These methods use the incremental cash flows from each potential investment, or project. Techniques based on accounting earnings and accounting rules are sometimes used - though economists consider this to be improper - such as the accounting rate of return, and 'return on investment.' Simplified and hybrid methods are used as well, such as payback period and discounted payback period.

a. Cash flow
b. Preferred stock
c. Gross profit
d. Capital Budgeting

18. _____ is that which is owed; usually referencing assets owed, but the term can also cover moral obligations and other interactions not requiring money. In the case of assets, _____ is a means of using future purchasing power in the present before a summation has been earned. Some companies and corporations use _____ as a part of their overall corporate finance strategy.

a. Debenture
b. Lender
c. Debt
d. Loan

19. A _____ is a fund established by a government agency or business for the purpose of reducing debt.

The _____ was first used in Great Britain in the 18th century to reduce national debt. While used by Robert Walpole in 1716 and effectively in the 1720s and early 1730s, it originated in the commercial tax syndicates of the Italian peninsula of the 14th century to retire redeemable public debt of those cities.

a. Treasury company
b. Segregated portfolio company
c. Payback period
d. Sinking fund

20. The term _____ or superannuation refers to a pension granted upon retirement. They may be set up by employers, insurance companies, the government or other institutions such as employer associations or trade unions.
a. Retirement plan
b. BMC Software, Inc.
c. Wage
d. 3M Company

21. An _____ is a company whose main business is holding securities of other companies purely for investment purposes. The _____ invests money on behalf of its shareholders who in turn share in the profits and losses.

In United States securities law, there are at least three types of investment companies :

- Open-End Management Investment Companies (mutual funds)
- Closed-End Management Investment Companies (closed-end funds)
- UITs (unit investment trusts)

A fourth and lesser-known type of _____ under the _____ Act of 1940 is a Face-Amount Certificate Company.

a. AIG
b. AMEX
c. ABC Television Network
d. Investment Company

22. The _____ is an act of Congress. It was passed as a United States Public Law (PL-768) on August 22, 1940, and is codified at 15 U.S.C. § 80a-1 through 15 U.S.C.

a. AIG
b. ABC Television Network
c. Investment Company Act of 1940
d. AMEX

23. An _____ is a term used in behavioral economics to describe those types of behaviors that impose costs on a person in the long-run that are not taken into account when making decisions in the present. Classical Economics discourages government from creating legislation that targets internalities, because it is assumed that the consumer takes these personal costs into account when paying for the good that causes the _____. For example, cigarettes should be taxed because of the negative consumption externalities that they impose, such as second-hand smoke, not because the smoker harms him or herself by smoking.

a. Internality
b. Operating budget
c. Inventory turnover ratio
d. Authorised capital

24. Net income is informally called the _____ because it is typically found on the last line of a company's income statement. A related term is top line, meaning revenue, which forms the first line of the account statement.

An equation for net income in merchandising:

Net income or net loss = Revenue - Cost of goods sold - Sales discounts - Sales returns and allowances - Expenses - Minority interest - Preferred stock dividends

a. Bottom line
b. Pro forma
c. Payroll
d. Current asset

Chapter 8. State and Local Government Accounting

25. _____ is the term used to refer to the standard framework of guidelines for financial accounting used in any given jurisdiction. _____ includes the standards, conventions, and rules accountants follow in recording and summarizing transactions, and in the preparation of financial statements.

Financial accounting information must be assembled and reported objectively.

a. Long-term liabilities
b. General ledger
c. Generally accepted accounting principles
d. Current asset

26. In finance, a _____ is a debt security, in which the authorized issuer owes the holders a debt and, depending on the terms of the _____, is obliged to pay interest (the coupon) and/or to repay the principal at a later date, termed maturity. It is a formal contract to repay borrowed money with interest at fixed intervals.

Thus a _____ is like a loan: the issuer is the borrower, the _____ holder is the lender, and the coupon is the interest.

a. Coupon rate
b. Revenue bonds
c. Zero-coupon bond
d. Bond

27. _____, Gross profit margin or Gross Profit Rate can be defined as the amount of contribution to the business enterprise, after paying for direct-fixed and direct-variable unit costs, required to cover overheads (fixed commitments) and provide a buffer for unknown items. It expresses the relationship between gross profit and sales revenue.

It can be expressed in absolute terms:

Gross Profit = Revenue − Cost of Goods Sold

or as the ratio of gross profit to sales revenue, usually in the form of a percentage:

_____ Percentage = (Revenue-Cost of Goods Sold)/Revenue

Cost of goods sold includes variable costs and fixed costs directly linked to the product, such as material and labor.

a. 3M Company
b. Gross margin
c. BNSF Railway
d. BMC Software, Inc.

Chapter 9. Implementation

1. In economics, a _____ is a mechanism that allows people to easily buy and sell (trade) financial securities (such as stocks and bonds), commodities (such as precious metals or agricultural goods), and other fungible items of value at low transaction costs and at prices that reflect the efficient-market hypothesis.

   They have evolved significantly over several hundred years and are undergoing constant innovation to improve liquidity.

   Both general markets (where many commodities are traded) and specialized markets (where only one commodity is traded) exist.

   a. Financial Market
   b. Spot rate
   c. Transfer agent
   d. Mark-to-market

2. A _____ is any one of a variety of different systems, institutions, procedures, social relations and infrastructures whereby persons trade, and goods and services are exchanged, forming part of the economy. It is an arrangement that allows buyers and sellers to exchange things. _____s vary in size, range, geographic scale, location, types and variety of human communities, as well as the types of goods and services traded.
   a. Perfect competition
   b. Market Failure
   c. Market
   d. Recession

3. In finance, or business _____ is the ability of an entity to pay its debts with available cash. _____ can also be described as the ability of a corporation to meet its long-term fixed expenses and to accomplish long-term expansion and growth. The better a company's _____, the better it is financially.
   a. 3M Company
   b. BMC Software, Inc.
   c. Solvency
   d. Capital asset

4. _____, the Electronic Data-Gathering, Analysis, and Retrieval system, performs automated collection, validation, indexing, acceptance, and forwarding of submissions by companies and others who are required by law to file forms with the U.S. Securities and Exchange Commission (the 'SEC'.) The database is freely available to the public via Web or FTP, typically posting in excess of 3,000 filings per day.

   Not all SEC filings by public companies are available on _____.

Chapter 9. Implementation

   a. AMEX
   b. EDGAR
   c. ABC Television Network
   d. AIG

5. _____ is a strategic management responsibility that integrates finance, communication, marketing and securities law compliance to enable the most effective two-way communication between a company, the financial community, and other constituencies, which ultimately contributes to a company's securities achieving fair valuation. The term describes the department of a company devoted to handling inquiries from shareholders and investors, as well as others who might be interested in a company's stock or financial stability.
   a. Investor Relations
   b. AIG
   c. AMEX
   d. ABC Television Network

6. In economics, _____ or _____ goods or real _____ refers to factors of production used to create goods or services that are not themselves significantly consumed (though they may depreciate) in the production process. _____ goods may be acquired with money or financial _____. In finance and accounting, _____ generally refers to financial wealth, especially that used to start or maintain a business.
   a. Vyborg Appeal
   b. Disclosure
   c. Screening
   d. Capital

7. In economics, business, retail, and accounting, a _____ is the value of money that has been used up to produce something, and hence is not available for use anymore. In economics, a _____ is an alternative that is given up as a result of a decision. In business, the _____ may be one of acquisition, in which case the amount of money expended to acquire it is counted as _____.
   a. Cost of quality
   b. Prime cost
   c. Cost
   d. Cost allocation

8. _____ is equal to the income that a firm has after subtracting costs and expenses from the total revenue. _____ can be distributed among holders of common stock as a dividend or held by the firm as retained earnings.

The items deducted will typically include tax expense, financing expense (interest expense), and minority interest. Likewise, preferred stock dividends will be subtracted too, though they are not an expense.

Chapter 9. Implementation

a. Generally accepted accounting principles
b. Matching principle
c. Long-term liabilities
d. Net income

9. _____ is an open standard which supports information modeling and the expression of semantic meaning commonly required in business reporting. _____ is XML-based. It uses the XML syntax and related XML technologies such as XML Schema, XLink, XPath, and Namespaces to articulate this semantic meaning. One use of _____ is to define and exchange financial information, such as a financial statement.
   a. BMC Software, Inc.
   b. 3M Company
   c. BNSF Railway
   d. XBRL

10. A _____ is a fungible, negotiable instrument representing financial value. they are broadly categorized into debt securities (such as banknotes, bonds and debentures), and equity securities; e.g., common stocks. The company or other entity issuing the _____ is called the issuer.
   a. Tracking stock
   b. Security
   c. 3M Company
   d. BMC Software, Inc.

11. The U.S. _____ is an independent agency of the United States government which holds primary responsibility for enforcing the federal securities laws and regulating the securities industry, the nation's stock and options exchanges, and other electronic securities markets. The SEC was created by section 4 of the Securities Exchange Act of 1934 (now codified as 15 U.S.C. §Â§ 78d and commonly referred to as the 1934 Act.)
   a. BMC Software, Inc.
   b. BNSF Railway
   c. 3M Company
   d. Securities and Exchange Commission

12. _____ is a list of the accounts including a unique number of each allowing to locate it in each ledger. The list is typically arranged in the order of the customary appearance of accounts in the financial statements. A _____ can track a specific financial information.

a. Journal entry
b. General journal
c. Chart of accounts
d. General ledger

13. The _____ is currently the source of generally accepted accounting principles (GAAP) used by State and Local governments in the [[United States of America]]. As with most of the entities involved in creating GAAP in the United States, it is a private, non-governmental organization.

The _____ is subject to oversight by the Financial Accounting Foundation (FAF), which selects the members of the _____ and the Financial Accounting Standards Board, and funds both organizations.

a. Fannie Mae
b. Governmental Accounting Standards Board
c. National Conference of Commissioners on Uniform State Laws
d. Multinational corporation

14. In financial accounting, a _____ or statement of financial position is a summary of a person's or organization's balances. Assets, liabilities and ownership equity are listed as of a specific date, such as the end of its financial year. A _____ is often described as a snapshot of a company's financial condition.

a. Financial statements
b. Statement of retained earnings
c. 3M Company
d. Balance sheet

15. _____ is the balance of the amounts of cash being received and paid by a business during a defined period of time, sometimes tied to a specific project. Measurement of _____ can be used

- to evaluate the state or performance of a business or project.
- to determine problems with liquidity. Being profitable does not necessarily mean being liquid. A company can fail because of a shortage of cash, even while profitable.
- to project rate of returns. The time of _____ s into and out of projects are used as inputs to financial models such as internal rate of return, and net present value.
- to examine income or growth of a business when it is believed that accrual accounting concepts do not represent economic realities. Alternately, _____ can be used to 'validate' the net income generated by accrual accounting.

_____ as a generic term may be used differently depending on context, and certain _____ definitions may be adapted by analysts and users for their own uses. Common terms include operating _____ and free _____.

a. Flow-through entity
b. Controlling interest
c. Commercial paper
d. Cash flow

16. In financial accounting, a _____ or Statement of cash flows is a financial statement that shows a company's flow of cash. The money coming into the business is called cash inflow, and money going out from the business is called cash outflow. The statement shows how changes in balance sheet and income accounts affect cash and cash equivalents, and breaks the analysis down to operating, investing, and financing activities.

a. BMC Software, Inc.
b. 3M Company
c. BNSF Railway
d. Cash flow statement

17. _____ are formal records of a business' financial activities.

In British English, including United Kingdom company law, _____ are often referred to as accounts, although the term _____ is also used, particularly by accountants.

_____ provide an overview of a business' financial condition in both short and long term.

a. Statement of retained earnings
b. Notes to the financial statements
c. 3M Company
d. Financial statements

18. _____ is the term used to refer to the standard framework of guidelines for financial accounting used in any given jurisdiction. _____ includes the standards, conventions, and rules accountants follow in recording and summarizing transactions, and in the preparation of financial statements.

Financial accounting information must be assembled and reported objectively.

a. Long-term liabilities
b. Generally accepted accounting principles
c. General ledger
d. Current asset

Chapter 9. Implementation

19. The _____ is the former authoritative body of the American Institute of Certified Public Accountants (AICPA.) It was created by the American Institute of Certified Public Accountants in 1959 and issued pronouncements on accounting principles until 1973, when it was replaced by the Financial Accounting Standards Board (FASB.)

The _____ was disbanded in the hopes that the smaller, fully-independent FASB could more effectively create accounting standards.

   a. American Payroll Association
   b. Accounting Principles Board
   c. Institute of Management Accountants
   d. International Federation of Accountants

20. The _____ is a private, not-for-profit organization whose primary purpose is to develop generally accepted accounting principles (GAAP) within the United States in the public's interest. The Securities and Exchange Commission (SEC) designated the _____ as the organization responsible for setting accounting standards for public companies in the U.S. It was created in 1973, replacing the Accounting Principles Board and the Committee on Accounting Procedure of the American Institute of Certified Public Accountants. The _____'s mission is 'to establish and improve standards of financial accounting and reporting for the guidance and education of the public, including issuers, auditors, and users of financial information.'

The _____ is not a governmental body.

   a. Governmental Accounting Standards Board
   b. Fannie Mae
   c. Public company
   d. Financial Accounting Standards Board

21. _____ is an umbrella term which refers to the various accounting systems used by various public sector entities. In the United States, for instance, there are two levels of government which follow different accounting standards set forth by independent, private sector boards. At the federal level, the Federal Accounting Standards Advisory Board (FASAB) sets forth the accounting standards to follow.
   a. Product control
   b. Management accounting
   c. Nonassurance services
   d. Governmental Accounting

22. The _____ was a predecessor of the Accounting Principles Board, itself a predecessor to the Financial Accounting Standards Board in the United States. Its formation and activities were early efforts to rationalize and legitimize the reporting of business performance. However, it is widely regarded as having failed.

Chapter 9. Implementation 89

a. Price variance
b. Consolidated financial statements
c. Lump sum
d. Committee on Accounting Procedure

23. _____ is a specific term used in companies' financial reporting from the company-whole point of view. Because that use excludes the effects of changing ownership interest, an economic measure of _____ is necessary for financial analysis from the shareholders' point of view

_____ is defined by the Financial Accounting Standards Board, or FASB, as 'the change in equity [net assets] of a business enterprise during a period from transactions and other events and circumstances from nonowner sources. It includes all changes in equity during a period except those resulting from investments by owners and distributions to owners.'

_____ is the sum of net income and other items that must bypass the income statement because they have not been realized, including items like an unrealized holding gain or loss from available for sale securities and foreign currency translation gains or losses.

a. BNSF Railway
b. Comprehensive income
c. BMC Software, Inc.
d. 3M Company

24. An _____ is a practitioner of accountancy, which is the measurement, disclosure or provision of assurance about financial information that helps managers, investors, tax authorities and other decision makers make resource allocation decisions.

The word '_____' is derived from the French 'Compter' which took its origin from the Latin 'Computare'. The word was formerly written in English as 'Accomptant', but in process of time the word, which was always pronounced by dropping the 'p', became gradually changed both in pronunciation and in orthography to its present form.

a. AMEX
b. Accountant
c. ABC Television Network
d. AIG

Chapter 9. Implementation

25. The _____ is the national, professional association of CPAs in the United States, with more than 330,000 members, including CPAs in business and industry, public practice, government, and education; student affiliates; and international associates. It sets ethical standards for the profession and U.S. auditing standards for audits of private companies; federal, state and local governments; and non-profit organizations.

Approximately 40% of its members are engaged in the practice of public accounting, in areas such as auditing, accounting, taxation, general business consulting, business valuation, personal financial planning and business technology.

   a. Other postemployment benefits
   b. ABC Television Network
   c. AIG
   d. American Institute of Certified Public Accountants

26. _____ is the statutory title of qualified accountants in the United States who have passed the Uniform _____ Examination and have met additional state education and experience requirements for certification as a _____. Individuals who have passed the Exam but have not either accomplished the required on-the-job experience or have previously met it but in the meantime have lapsed their continuing professional education are, in many states, permitted the designation '_____ Inactive' or an equivalent phrase. In most U.S. states, only _____s who are licensed are able to provide to the public attestation (including auditing) opinions on financial statements.
   a. Certified Public Accountant
   b. Chartered Accountant
   c. Certified General Accountant
   d. Chartered Certified Accountant

27. The _____ of 2002 (Pub.L. 107-204, 116 Stat. 745, enacted July 30, 2002), also known as the Public Company Accounting Reform and Investor Protection Act of 2002, is a United States federal law enacted on July 30, 2002 in response to a number of major corporate and accounting scandals including those affecting Enron, Tyco International, Adelphia, Peregrine Systems and WorldCom. The legislation establishes new or enhanced standards for all U.S. public company boards, management, and public accounting firms. It does not apply to privately held companies.
   a. FCPA
   b. Fair Labor Standards Act
   c. Lease
   d. Sarbanes-Oxley Act

28. The term '_____' refers to the concept of collecting information and attempting to spot a pattern in the information. In some fields of study, the term '_____' has more formally-defined meanings.

In project management _____ is a mathematical technique that uses historical results to predict future outcome.

a. Multicollinearity
b. Trend analysis
c. 3M Company
d. Regression analysis

29. An _____ is the buying of one company by another. An _____ may be friendly or hostile. In the former case, the companies cooperate in negotiations; in the latter case, the takeover target is unwilling to be bought or the target's board has no prior knowledge of the offer. _____ usually refers to a purchase of a smaller firm by a larger one. Sometimes, however, a smaller firm will acquire management control of a larger or longer established company and keep its name for the combined entity. This is known as a reverse takeover.
   a. Acquisition
   b. ABC Television Network
   c. AMEX
   d. AIG

30. In business and accounting, _____ are everything of value that is owned by a person or company. It is a claim on the property your income of a borrower. The balance sheet of a firm records the monetary value of the _____ owned by the firm.
   a. Assets
   b. Accrual basis accounting
   c. Accounts receivable
   d. Earnings before interest, taxes, depreciation and amortization

31. _____, also called fair price (in a commonplace conflation of the two distinct concepts), is a concept used in finance and economics, defined as a rational and unbiased estimate of the potential market price of a good, service, or asset, taking into account such objective factors as:

- acquisition/production/distribution costs, replacement costs, or costs of close substitutes
- actual utility at a given level of development of social productive capability
- supply vs. demand

and subjective factors such as

- risk characteristics
- cost of capital
- individually perceived utility

Chapter 9. Implementation

In accounting, _____ is used as an estimate of the market value of an asset (or liability) for which a market price cannot be determined (usually because there is no established market for the asset.) Under GAAP (FAS 157), _____ is the amount at which the asset could be bought or sold in a current transaction between willing parties, or transferred to an equivalent party, other than in a liquidation sale. This is used for assets whose carrying value is based on mark-to-market valuations; for assets carried at historical cost, the _____ of the asset is not used. One example of where _____ is an issue is a College kitchen with a cost of $2 million which was built 5 years ago.

a. Fair value
b. BMC Software, Inc.
c. BNSF Railway
d. 3M Company

32. _____ are defined as identifiable non-monetary assets that cannot be seen, touched or physically measured, which are created through time and/or effort and that are identifiable as a separate asset. There are two primary forms of intangibles - legal intangibles (such as trade secrets (e.g., customer lists), copyrights, patents, trademarks, and goodwill) and competitive intangibles (such as knowledge activities (know-how, knowledge), collaboration activities, leverage activities, and structural activities.) Legal intangibles are known under the generic term intellectual property and generate legal property rights defensible in a court of law.

a. Overhead
b. ABC Television Network
c. AIG
d. Intangible assets

33. In financial accounting, a _____ is defined as an obligation of an entity arising from past transactions or events, the settlement of which may result in the transfer or use of assets, provision of services or other yielding of economic benefits in the future.

a. Vested
b. Corporate governance
c. False Claims Act
d. Liability

34. In finance, an _____ is a contract between a buyer and a seller that gives the buyer the right--but not the obligation--to buy or to sell a particular asset (the underlying asset) at a later time at an agreed price. In return for granting the _____, the seller collects a payment (the premium) from the buyer. A call _____ gives the buyer the right to buy the underlying asset; a put _____ gives the buyer of the _____ the right to sell the underlying asset.

a. Option
b. ABC Television Network
c. AMEX
d. AIG

35. A _____, (formerly a securities exchange) is a corporation or mutual organization which provides 'trading' facilities for stock brokers and traders, to trade stocks and other securities. _____s also provide facilities for the issue and redemption of securities as well as other financial instruments and capital events including the payment of income and dividends. The securities traded on a _____ include: shares issued by companies, unit trusts, derivatives, pooled investment products and bonds.
   a. BNSF Railway
   b. Stock exchange
   c. BMC Software, Inc.
   d. 3M Company

36. The _____ is located in Norwalk, Connecticut. It is an independent, organization in the private sector that is responsible for oversight of the Financial Accounting Standards Board (FASB), the Governmental Accounting Standards Board (GASB), and their respective advisory councils.
   a. Financial Accounting Foundation
   b. BNSF Railway
   c. 3M Company
   d. BMC Software, Inc.

37. The _____ founded on April 1, 2001 is the successor of the International Accounting Standards Committee (IASC) founded in June 1973 in London. It is responsible for developing the International Financial Reporting Standards (new name for the International Accounting Standards issued after 2001), and promoting the use and application of these standards.

The _____ is an independent, privately-funded accounting standard-setter based in London, UK.

   a. Institute of Management Accountants
   b. Information Systems Audit and Control Association
   c. Emerging technologies
   d. International Accounting Standards Board

38. The term _____ usually refers to a company that is permitted to offer its registered securities (stock, bonds, etc.) for sale to the general public, typically through a stock exchange, or occasionally a company whose stock is traded over the counter (OTC) via market makers who use non-exchange quotation services.

The term '_____' may also refer to a company owned by the government.

a. Governmental Accounting Standards Board
b. MicroStrategy
c. Professional association
d. Public Company

39. The _____ (sometimes called 'Peekaboo') is a private-sector, non-profit corporation created by the Sarbanes-Oxley Act, a 2002 United States federal law, to oversee the auditors of public companies. Its stated purpose is to 'protect the interests of investors and further the public interest in the preparation of informative, fair, and independent audit reports'. Although a private entity, the _____ has many government-like regulatory functions, making it in some ways similar to the private Self Regulatory Organizations (SROs) that regulate stock markets and other aspects of the financial markets in the United States.

a. 3M Company
b. Financial Crimes Enforcement Network
c. Pension Benefit Guaranty Corporation
d. Public Company Accounting Oversight Board

40. The general definition of an _____ is an evaluation of a person, organization, system, process, project or product. _____s are performed to ascertain the validity and reliability of information; also to provide an assessment of a system's internal control. The goal of an _____ is to express an opinion on the person/organization/system (etc) in question, under evaluation based on work done on a test basis.

a. Audit regime
b. Assurance service
c. Institute of Chartered Accountants of India
d. Audit

Chapter 10. Federal Accounting Standards

1. The _____ is a private, not-for-profit organization whose primary purpose is to develop generally accepted accounting principles (GAAP) within the United States in the public's interest. The Securities and Exchange Commission (SEC) designated the _____ as the organization responsible for setting accounting standards for public companies in the U.S. It was created in 1973, replacing the Accounting Principles Board and the Committee on Accounting Procedure of the American Institute of Certified Public Accountants. The _____'s mission is 'to establish and improve standards of financial accounting and reporting for the guidance and education of the public, including issuers, auditors, and users of financial information.'

The _____ is not a governmental body.

   a. Fannie Mae
   b. Governmental Accounting Standards Board
   c. Financial Accounting Standards Board
   d. Public company

2. _____ is the act of taking possession of or assigning purpose to properties or ideas and is important in many topics, including:

   - _____ in relation to the spread of knowledge
   - _____ (art)
     - _____ (music) in reference to the re-use and proliferation of different types of music
   - _____ (economics) origination of human ownership of previously unowned natural resources such as land
   - _____ (law) as a component of government spending
   - Cultural _____ is the borrowing, or theft, of an element of cultural expression of one group by another.
   - The tort of _____ is one form of invasion of privacy.

   a. Improvement
   b. Annuity
   c. Intangible
   d. Appropriation

3. In accounting, _____ has a very specific meaning. It is an outflow of cash or other valuable assets from a person or company to another person or company. This outflow of cash is generally one side of a trade for products or services that have equal or better current or future value to the buyer than to the seller.
   a. AMEX
   b. ABC Television Network
   c. Expense
   d. AIG

Chapter 10. Federal Accounting Standards

4. In economics, _____ or _____ goods or real _____ refers to factors of production used to create goods or services that are not themselves significantly consumed (though they may depreciate) in the production process. _____ goods may be acquired with money or financial _____. In finance and accounting, _____ generally refers to financial wealth, especially that used to start or maintain a business.
   a. Disclosure
   b. Vyborg Appeal
   c. Capital
   d. Screening

5. _____ is a financial metric which represents operating liquidity available to a business. Along with fixed assets such as plant and equipment, _____ is considered a part of operating capital. It is calculated as current assets minus current liabilities.
   a. Working capital management
   b. BMC Software, Inc.
   c. Working capital
   d. 3M Company

6. The _____ was established as the _____ by the Budget and Accounting Act of 1921 (Pub.L. 67-13, 42 Stat. 20, June 10, 1921.)
   a. 3M Company
   b. GAO
   c. BMC Software, Inc.
   d. General Accounting Office

7. An _____ is a practitioner of accountancy, which is the measurement, disclosure or provision of assurance about financial information that helps managers, investors, tax authorities and other decision makers make resource allocation decisions.

The word '_____' is derived from the French 'Compter' which took its origin from the Latin 'Computare'. The word was formerly written in English as 'Accomptant', but in process of time the word, which was always pronounced by dropping the 'p', became gradually changed both in pronunciation and in orthography to its present form.

   a. AIG
   b. AMEX
   c. ABC Television Network
   d. Accountant

Chapter 10. Federal Accounting Standards

8. Project _____: The project _____ is a prediction of the costs associated with a particular company project. These costs include labor, materials, and other related expenses. The project _____ is often broken down into specific tasks, with task _____s assigned to each.
   a. 3M Company
   b. BMC Software, Inc.
   c. BNSF Railway
   d. Budget

9. The _____ is a Cabinet-level office, and is the largest office within the Executive Office of the President of the United States (EOP.) It is an important conduit by which the White House oversees the activities of federal agencies. OMB is tasked with giving expert advice to senior White House officials on a range of topics relating to federal policy, management, legislative, regulatory, and budgetary issues.
   a. Analysis of variance
   b. AT'T Wireless Services, Inc.
   c. Alaska Air Group
   d. Office of Management and Budget

10. In accounting, _____ or carrying value is the value of an asset according to its balance sheet account balance. For assets, the value is based on the original cost of the asset less any depreciation, amortization or impairment costs made against the asset. Traditionally, a company's _____ is its total assets minus intangible assets and liabilities.
    a. Matching principle
    b. Depreciation
    c. Generally accepted accounting principles
    d. Book value

11. In business and accounting, _____ are everything of value that is owned by a person or company. It is a claim on the property your income of a borrower. The balance sheet of a firm records the monetary value of the _____ owned by the firm.
    a. Accounts receivable
    b. Earnings before interest, taxes, depreciation and amortization
    c. Accrual basis accounting
    d. Assets

12. _____, in accrual accounting, is any account where the asset or liability is not realized until a future date (accounting period), e.g. annuities, charges, taxes, income, etc. The _____ item may be carried, dependent on type of deferral, as either an asset or liability.

a. Payroll
b. Pro forma
c. Cash basis accounting
d. Deferred

13. _____ is the practice of postponing maintenance activities such as repairs on both real property (i.e. infrastructure) and personal property (i.e. machinery) in order to save costs, meet budget funding levels, or realign available budget monies. The failure to perform needed repairs could lead to asset deterioration and ultimately asset impairment. Generally, a policy of continued _____ may result in higher costs, asset failure, and in some cases, health and safety implications.
    a. BNSF Railway
    b. BMC Software, Inc.
    c. 3M Company
    d. Deferred maintenance

14. In economics, business, retail, and accounting, a _____ is the value of money that has been used up to produce something, and hence is not available for use anymore. In economics, a _____ is an alternative that is given up as a result of a decision. In business, the _____ may be one of acquisition, in which case the amount of money expended to acquire it is counted as _____.
    a. Cost allocation
    b. Cost
    c. Prime cost
    d. Cost of quality

15. In management accounting, _____ establishes budget and actual cost of operations, processes, departments or product and the analysis of variances, profitability or social use of funds. Managers use _____ to support decision-making to cut a company's costs and improve profitability. As a form of management accounting, _____ need not follow standards such as GAAP, because its primary use is for internal managers, rather than outside users, and what to compute is instead decided pragmatically.
    a. Cost accounting
    b. Cost-volume-profit analysis
    c. Prime cost
    d. Marginal cost

16. _____ is concerned with the provisions and use of accounting information to managers within organizations, to provide them with the basis to make informed business decisions that will allow them to be better equipped in their management and control functions.

Chapter 10. Federal Accounting Standards

In contrast to financial accountancy information, _____ information is:

- usually confidential and used by management, instead of publicly reported;
- forward-looking, instead of historical;
- pragmatically computed using extensive management information systems and internal controls, instead of complying with accounting standards.

This is because of the different emphasis: _____ information is used within an organization, typically for decision-making.

a. Governmental accounting
b. Nonassurance services
c. Management accounting
d. Grenzplankostenrechnung

Chapter 11. Summary of Recommendations

1. The _____ is a private, not-for-profit organization whose primary purpose is to develop generally accepted accounting principles (GAAP) within the United States in the public's interest. The Securities and Exchange Commission (SEC) designated the _____ as the organization responsible for setting accounting standards for public companies in the U.S. It was created in 1973, replacing the Accounting Principles Board and the Committee on Accounting Procedure of the American Institute of Certified Public Accountants. The _____'s mission is 'to establish and improve standards of financial accounting and reporting for the guidance and education of the public, including issuers, auditors, and users of financial information.'

The _____ is not a governmental body.

   a. Fannie Mae
   b. Public company
   c. Governmental Accounting Standards Board
   d. Financial Accounting Standards Board

2. In economics, a _____ is a mechanism that allows people to easily buy and sell (trade) financial securities (such as stocks and bonds), commodities (such as precious metals or agricultural goods), and other fungible items of value at low transaction costs and at prices that reflect the efficient-market hypothesis.

They have evolved significantly over several hundred years and are undergoing constant innovation to improve liquidity.

Both general markets (where many commodities are traded) and specialized markets (where only one commodity is traded) exist.

   a. Financial Market
   b. Spot rate
   c. Transfer agent
   d. Mark-to-market

3. _____ is an umbrella term which refers to the various accounting systems used by various public sector entities. In the United States, for instance, there are two levels of government which follow different accounting standards set forth by independent, private sector boards. At the federal level, the Federal Accounting Standards Advisory Board (FASAB) sets forth the accounting standards to follow.
   a. Nonassurance services
   b. Product control
   c. Governmental Accounting
   d. Management accounting

Chapter 11. Summary of Recommendations

4. The _____ is currently the source of generally accepted accounting principles (GAAP) used by State and Local governments in the [[United States of America]]. As with most of the entities involved in creating GAAP in the United States, it is a private, non-governmental organization.

The _____ is subject to oversight by the Financial Accounting Foundation (FAF), which selects the members of the _____ and the Financial Accounting Standards Board, and funds both organizations.

   a. Multinational corporation
   b. National Conference of Commissioners on Uniform State Laws
   c. Fannie Mae
   d. Governmental Accounting Standards Board

5. A _____ is any one of a variety of different systems, institutions, procedures, social relations and infrastructures whereby persons trade, and goods and services are exchanged, forming part of the economy. It is an arrangement that allows buyers and sellers to exchange things. _____s vary in size, range, geographic scale, location, types and variety of human communities, as well as the types of goods and services traded.

   a. Market Failure
   b. Recession
   c. Perfect competition
   d. Market

6. In financial accounting, a _____ or statement of financial position is a summary of a person's or organization's balances. Assets, liabilities and ownership equity are listed as of a specific date, such as the end of its financial year. A _____ is often described as a snapshot of a company's financial condition.

   a. Statement of retained earnings
   b. Financial statements
   c. 3M Company
   d. Balance sheet

7. In finance, or business _____ is the ability of an entity to pay its debts with available cash. _____ can also be described as the ability of a corporation to meet its long-term fixed expenses and to accomplish long-term expansion and growth. The better a company's _____, the better it is financially.

   a. Solvency
   b. BMC Software, Inc.
   c. 3M Company
   d. Capital asset

Chapter 11. Summary of Recommendations

8. _____ is an open standard which supports information modeling and the expression of semantic meaning commonly required in business reporting. _____ is XML-based. It uses the XML syntax and related XML technologies such as XML Schema, XLink, XPath, and Namespaces to articulate this semantic meaning. One use of _____ is to define and exchange financial information, such as a financial statement.
   a. BMC Software, Inc.
   b. 3M Company
   c. XBRL
   d. BNSF Railway

9. _____ is the balance of the amounts of cash being received and paid by a business during a defined period of time, sometimes tied to a specific project. Measurement of _____ can be used

   - to evaluate the state or performance of a business or project.
   - to determine problems with liquidity. Being profitable does not necessarily mean being liquid. A company can fail because of a shortage of cash, even while profitable.
   - to project rate of returns. The time of _____s into and out of projects are used as inputs to financial models such as internal rate of return, and net present value.
   - to examine income or growth of a business when it is believed that accrual accounting concepts do not represent economic realities. Alternately, _____ can be used to 'validate' the net income generated by accrual accounting.

   _____ as a generic term may be used differently depending on context, and certain _____ definitions may be adapted by analysts and users for their own uses. Common terms include operating _____ and free _____.

   a. Controlling interest
   b. Cash flow
   c. Flow-through entity
   d. Commercial paper

10. In financial accounting, a _____ or Statement of cash flows is a financial statement that shows a company's flow of cash. The money coming into the business is called cash inflow, and money going out from the business is called cash outflow. The statement shows how changes in balance sheet and income accounts affect cash and cash equivalents, and breaks the analysis down to operating, investing, and financing activities.
    a. Cash flow statement
    b. BMC Software, Inc.
    c. 3M Company
    d. BNSF Railway

Chapter 11. Summary of Recommendations

11. In economics, business, retail, and accounting, a _____ is the value of money that has been used up to produce something, and hence is not available for use anymore. In economics, a _____ is an alternative that is given up as a result of a decision. In business, the _____ may be one of acquisition, in which case the amount of money expended to acquire it is counted as _____.

   a. Cost allocation
   b. Cost of quality
   c. Prime cost
   d. Cost

12. In financial accounting, _____ , cash flow provided by operations or cash flow from operating activities, refers to the amount of cash a company generates from the revenues it brings in, excluding costs associated with long-term investment on capital items or investment in securities.

   _____ = Cash generated from operations less taxation and interest paid, investment income received and less dividends paid gives rise to _____s per International Financial Reporting Standards.

   To calculate cash generated from operations, one must calculate cash generated from customers and cash paid to suppliers.

   a. AIG
   b. AMEX
   c. ABC Television Network
   d. Operating cash flow

13. The _____ founded on April 1, 2001 is the successor of the International Accounting Standards Committee (IASC) founded in June 1973 in London. It is responsible for developing the International Financial Reporting Standards (new name for the International Accounting Standards issued after 2001), and promoting the use and application of these standards.

   The _____ is an independent, privately-funded accounting standard-setter based in London, UK.

   a. Information Systems Audit and Control Association
   b. Emerging technologies
   c. Institute of Management Accountants
   d. International Accounting Standards Board

14. The term _____ usually refers to a company that is permitted to offer its registered securities (stock, bonds, etc.) for sale to the general public, typically through a stock exchange, or occasionally a company whose stock is traded over the counter (OTC) via market makers who use non-exchange quotation services.

   The term '_____' may also refer to a company owned by the government.

a. Public Company
b. Professional association
c. MicroStrategy
d. Governmental Accounting Standards Board

15. The _____ (sometimes called 'Peekaboo') is a private-sector, non-profit corporation created by the Sarbanes-Oxley Act, a 2002 United States federal law, to oversee the auditors of public companies. Its stated purpose is to 'protect the interests of investors and further the public interest in the preparation of informative, fair, and independent audit reports'. Although a private entity, the _____ has many government-like regulatory functions, making it in some ways similar to the private Self Regulatory Organizations (SROs) that regulate stock markets and other aspects of the financial markets in the United States.
a. Public Company Accounting Oversight Board
b. 3M Company
c. Pension Benefit Guaranty Corporation
d. Financial Crimes Enforcement Network

ANSWER KEY

Chapter 1
1. c	2. d	3. d	4. d	5. d	6. c	7. b	8. a	9. d	10. d
11. d	12. c	13. a	14. d	15. d	16. c	17. a	18. d	19. a	20. c
21. a	22. c	23. d	24. b	25. b	26. d	27. c	28. a	29. a	30. d
31. d	32. b	33. c	34. d	35. d	36. b	37. b	38. b	39. a	40. a
41. b	42. a	43. d	44. b	45. a	46. c				

Chapter 2
1. b	2. a	3. d	4. c	5. d	6. d	7. a	8. b	9. d	10. d
11. d	12. a	13. c	14. b	15. b	16. a	17. d	18. b	19. a	20. d
21. d	22. c	23. c	24. b	25. b	26. d	27. c	28. c	29. d	30. d
31. b	32. c	33. b	34. a	35. c					

Chapter 3
1. d	2. d	3. d	4. d	5. d	6. d	7. c	8. d	9. b	10. d
11. c	12. d	13. b	14. d	15. b	16. a	17. c	18. a	19. a	20. b
21. b	22. c	23. c	24. b	25. d	26. a	27. b	28. a	29. c	30. b
31. a	32. d	33. c	34. c	35. d	36. c	37. b	38. d	39. d	40. d
41. d	42. a	43. a	44. d	45. d	46. a	47. d	48. d	49. c	50. b
51. a	52. d	53. c	54. c	55. d	56. c	57. d	58. d	59. d	

Chapter 4
1. d	2. a	3. a	4. c	5. d	6. d	7. a	8. a	9. d	10. a
11. a	12. d	13. d	14. b	15. b	16. d	17. a	18. d	19. d	20. b
21. b	22. c	23. d	24. b	25. d	26. a	27. b	28. d	29. c	30. d
31. c	32. b	33. d	34. d	35. d					

Chapter 5
1. b	2. d	3. d	4. c	5. d	6. b	7. c	8. d	9. c	10. d
11. d	12. d	13. b	14. c	15. b	16. d				

Chapter 6
1. b	2. d	3. a	4. a	5. a	6. d	7. c	8. b	9. d	10. d
11. d	12. d	13. a	14. d	15. b					

Chapter 7
1. b	2. d	3. d	4. b	5. c	6. d	7. d	8. d	9. a	10. d
11. b	12. b	13. a	14. b	15. a	16. c				

Chapter 8
1. c	2. c	3. a	4. d	5. b	6. a	7. d	8. b	9. d	10. d
11. a	12. d	13. a	14. d	15. d	16. d	17. d	18. c	19. d	20. a
21. d	22. c	23. a	24. a	25. c	26. d	27. b			

ANSWER KEY

Chapter 9

1. a	2. c	3. c	4. b	5. a	6. d	7. c	8. d	9. d	10. b
11. d	12. c	13. b	14. d	15. d	16. d	17. d	18. b	19. b	20. d
21. d	22. d	23. b	24. b	25. d	26. a	27. d	28. b	29. a	30. a
31. a	32. d	33. d	34. a	35. b	36. a	37. d	38. d	39. d	40. d

Chapter 10

1. c	2. d	3. c	4. c	5. c	6. d	7. d	8. d	9. d	10. d
11. d	12. d	13. d	14. b	15. a	16. c				

Chapter 11

1. d	2. a	3. c	4. d	5. d	6. d	7. a	8. c	9. b	10. a
11. d	12. d	13. d	14. a	15. a